IDENTITY, LANGUAGE, AND MIND

IDENTITY, LANGUAGE, AND MIND

An Introduction to the Philosophy of JOHN PERRY

edited by

Albert Newen & Raphael van Riel

CSLI PUBLICATIONS
Center for the Study of
Language and Information
Stanford, California

mentis
Paderborn
Germany

CSLI Publications
Center for the Study of Language and Information
Leland Stanford Junior University
Printed in the United States
15 14 13 12   1 2 3 4 5

Library of Congress Cataloging-in-Publication Data

Identity, language, and mind : introduction to the philosophy of John Perry / edited by Albert Newen and Raphael van Riel.
p. cm. – (CSLI lecture notes ; no. 203)
Includes bibliographical references and index.
ISBN 978-1-57586-643-7 (cloth : alk. paper) –
ISBN 978-1-57586-642-0 (pbk. : alk. paper)
1. Perry, John, 1943- I. Newen, Albert. II. Riel, Raphael van, 1979-

B945.P454I34 2012
191–dc23

2011045906
CIP

CSLI Publications gratefully acknowledges a generous gift from Jill and Donald Knuth in support of scholarly publishing that has made the production of this book possible.

∞ The acid-free paper used in this book meets the minimum requirements of the American National Standard for Information Sciences—Permanence of Paper for Printed Library Materials, ANSI Z39.48-1984.

CSLI was founded in 1983 by researchers from Stanford University, SRI International, and Xerox PARC to further the research and development of integrated theories of language, information, and computation. CSLI headquarters and CSLI Publications are located on the campus of Stanford University.

CSLI Publications reports new developments in the study of language, information, and computation. Please visit our web site at
http://cslipublications.stanford.edu/
for comments on this and other titles, as well as for changes and corrections by the author and publisher.

Contents

Contributors

DANIEL COHNITZ: Department of Philosophy, University of Tartu, Ülikooli 18, 50090 Tartu, Estonia.
cohnitz@ut.ee

JEROME DOKIC: Institut Jean-Nicod, École Normale Supérieure, 29 rue d'Ulm, 75005 Paris, France.
dokic@ehess.fr

KEPA KORTA: ILCLI, UPV-EHU, Carlos Santamaria Zentroa, Elhuyar Plaza 2, 20018 Donostia, Spain.
kepa.korta@ehu.es

ALBERT NEWEN: Ruhr-Universität Bochum, Institut für Philosophie II, 44780 Bochum, Germany.
albert.newen@rub.de

ISIDORA STOJANOVIC: Institut Jean-Nicod, Ècole Normale Supérieure, 29 rue d'Ulm, 75005 Paris, France.
isidora.stojanovic@ens.fr

NEIL VAN LEEUWEN: Georgia State University, Department of Philosophy, Atlanta, Georgia 30302-4089, USA.
neilvl@gmail.com

RAPHAEL VAN RIEL: Ruhr-Universität Bochum, Institut für Philosophie II, 44780 Bochum, Germany.
raphael.vanriel@rub.de

Preface and Acknowledgements

One of the most famous stories in philosophy belongs to John Perry:

"I once followed a trail of sugar on a supermarket floor, pushing my cart down the aisle on one side of a tall counter and back the aisle on the other, seeking the shopper with the torn sack to tell him he was making a mess. With each trip around the counter, the trail became thicker. But I seemed unable to catch up. Finally it dawned on me. I was the shopper I was trying to catch."

It is typical for Perry that this is a story about an everyday situation (not a far-fetched fictional world) that at the same time nicely illustrates a core problem of modern philosophy, the problem of representing oneself with the use of "I" or in a self-reflexive way. The phenomena of self-consciousness, self-awareness, and self-knowledge in relation to the typical linguistic expressions form one of the main topics and a major starting point in Perry's work.

Our aim is to follow the trail of Perry's extensive work. Since he made important contributions to several topics in contemporary philosophy, this book can also serve as an introduction to central themes in philosophy of language and philosophy of mind. Moreover, we hope it gives insight into a specific approach to genuine contemporary analytic philosophy, which finds an elegant and striking expression in the works—writings as well as lectures—of John Perry. This approach is marked by three features: precision, clarity, and candor. The more than one hundred articles and books authored by Perry prove that these goals can be achieved with elegance and style. It is no wonder that John Perry inspired generations of students during his impressive career.

Having finished his PhD at Cornell University in 1968, he was appointed Assistant Professor at UCLA. At Stanford University, he became Associate Professor in 1974 and Full Professor in 1977. He also spent several months in 1971/72 as a Visiting Assistant Professor at the University of

Michigan, Ann Arbor. Perry has received many academic awards and also spent the academic years 1991/92 and 1999/2000 in Europe, first as a Visiting Fellow at the *Centre de Recherche en Epistémologie Appliquée* in Paris, where he delivered the Jean Nicod Lectures (Nicod Prize 1999), and then as a Humboldt Awardee (1999/2000) at the University of Bonn. Perry essentially initiated and formed the famous Center for the Study of Language and Information (CSLI) at Stanford University, and he is still one of the main figures in modern philosophy of mind and language.

The present volume picks up on seven central topics in the work of John Perry, which are grouped into two larger units. These units form the core parts of the volume. They are preceded by a chapter that introduces these topics and gives an idea of the relevant terminology. Each chapter is written by a philosopher who has worked on Perry's philosophy, and several contributors have even worked personally with Perry himself. The bibliographical part of this book contains, in addition to a list of cited works, an extended list of John Perry's philosophical publications. The first main part of this book, consisting of four chapters, is concerned with aspects of John Perry's work on themes from the philosophy of language: *indexicality*, *reference*, *propositional attitudes*, and *situation semantics*. This book's second part contains three chapters concerned with Perry's views on how a self can be situated in a physical world, where he discusses questions concerning *self-knowledge*, *personal identity*, and what he describes as *antecedent physicalism*. All chapters are written in a way that should make them accessible to students with little background in analytic philosophy. They will introduce the reader not only to the conceptual apparatus used and the main theses defended by Perry, but also to the broader topics themselves. Thus, we hope this book will achieve the goal of at least partly reflecting the richness of John Perry's work, as well as the influence it had in the past decades and, we are glad to say, still has in a number of interrelated branches of contemporary analytic philosophy.

Finally, we would like to thank all those who made the production of this book possible. Special thanks are due to Dikran Karagueuzian for his support and flexibility as Director of CSLI Publications. Furthermore, we would like to thank Lara Kirfel and Robert Schütze for their assistance in proof reading and formatting, Nadine Overkamp for her administrative assistance, and, especially, Neil Van Leeuwen, who not only contributed to the volume, but also polished the papers of those contributors who are non-native speakers.

Bochum, October 2011, Albert Newen and Raphael van Riel

1

Speaking and Thinking About Oneself with the Work of John Perry

ALBERT NEWEN AND RAPHAEL VAN RIEL

To gain access to the main aspects of Perry's work, we should take a look at both simple (extensional) sentences, such as "Snow is white", and at propositional attitude reports, such as "Peter believes that snow is white". Intuitively, propositional attitude reports connect the realm of language with that of thought; in sentences such as "Peter believes that snow is white", we describe a thought of Peter's using a declarative sentence, namely "Snow is white". In virtue of this fact, they can be used to illustrate the two main objectives of Perry's work, i.e. *understanding the semantics of natural language,* on the one hand, and *giving a thorough account of thoughts and of persons as mental beings,* on the other.

Suppose John Perry does not know that he is the philosopher this book is dedicated to. He knows that we intend to edit a volume on philosophy of language, but mistakenly thinks that it will be dedicated to John Searle. With this background, we may consider the following utterances:

(1) John Perry is a professor at Stanford University.
(2) The philosopher the edition by Newen and van Riel is dedicated to is professor at Stanford University.
(3) I am professor at Stanford University. (Uttered by John Perry)

All these sentences can be used to ascribe the property of being professor at Stanford University to John Perry, and they are true just in case John Perry is a professor at Stanford University. Now, consider how John Perry would

Identity, Language, and Mind: An Introduction to the Philosophy of John Perry.
Albert Newen and Raphael van Riel (eds.).

evaluate these sentences given the epistemic situation described above: He will evaluate the sentences (1) and (3) as true, but (2) as false (since he knows that John Searle is professor at the University of California at Berkeley). This is striking: How can that be, given that the expressions "John Perry", "The philosopher the edition of Newen and van Riel is dedicated to", and "I"—when uttered by Perry—refer to the same object, namely, John Perry? We can even modify the epistemic scenario so that John Perry—for a short period—is suffering from a severe amnesia and may have forgotten his name. Then he may only evaluate (3) as true, while (1) and (2) are taken to be false. Thus, the three sentences are epistemically distinct; one might say that they have distinct epistemic functions. This is closely connected with their evaluation as true and false. According to Perry all three utterances have a different *cognitive significance*. According to one tradition in the semantics of natural language, what Perry labels *cognitive significance* should be accounted for in a thorough account of meaning: Difference in meaning translates into difference in cognitive significance. But *should* a semantics of natural language account for cognitive significance, and if so, how could this be done? How can we account for the meaning of utterances containing the first person pronoun (as in 3)? These are the main questions the first part of the book deals with—these are questions from the philosophy of language. The bridge to the philosophy of mind can be illustrated by referring to propositional attitude reports.

On the basis of an utterance (3), we are justified in reporting John's belief as follows:

(4) John believes that he is a professor at Stanford University.

Using this sentence, we ascribe a *belief* to *John*, namely, the belief *that he is a professor at Stanford University*. This points to a number of central themes in modern analytic philosophy, and it also enables us to sketch the main topics of Perry's work and to highlight some of the interconnections between them. This can be done by giving a rough interpretation of the components of a propositional attitude report.

An ordinary propositional attitude report is expressed by a sentence that—at first glance—is concerned with (i) a person and a mental state of this person, which is characterized (ii) in terms of the relevant attitude (e.g. a belief, a desire, etc.), and (iii) in terms of this attitude's propositional content—referred to by the that-clause. Let us characterize these elements in more detail:

For (4) to be true, John must be capable of having mental states; in other words, (4) seems to commit its user to the assumption that John is a minded entity. Moreover, he belongs to a specific kind of minded entities:

He is a person. Persons are the subject of moral evaluations; it is persons whose epistemic states guide the interest in epistemology; and propositional attitude reports paradigmatically deal with persons. Thus, an understanding of what persons are is key to a number of different philosophical enterprises. In Perry's work, personhood is an important background topic; thus, he has worked out a general view of what it is for a person to exist over time.

A second topic in Perry's work can be characterized by the next constituent of (4): John is capable of having specific attitudes, for example, a belief. This is one attitude amongst others, such as desires, fears, and hopes, and it is just one sort of mental state amongst other sorts of mental states, such as phenomenal experience, perception, and raw feelings. This inspires questions concerning the metaphysics of the mind: What is it to possess a belief and other mental states in a world that contains physical entities only? This in turn connects with the debate whether mental entities can be adequately explained within a physicalist framework.

As a third feature of (4), we have the *content* of John's propositional attitude, which is referred to by the expression 'that he is a professor at Stanford University'. It has the function of delivering the same content as was expressed by the first person utterance (3). Given the specific cognitive dynamics of thoughts expressed using the pronoun "I" (de se thoughts), we are dealing with the specific demand to adequately characterize *the semantics of natural language expressions*, especially focusing on different types of coreferential singular terms, i.e. proper names, indexicals, and definite descriptions.

This gives an idea of the topics John Perry has worked on and of the structure of this volume: In the first part, Perry's important contributions concerning the semantics of natural language are presented, while the second part addresses central topics on persons as mental beings, including the structure of first-person thoughts, Perry's views on personal identity, and the nature of mental phenomena in a physical world.

The next two sections will introduce the basic framework of Perry's ideas and give a somewhat more detailed idea of the topics addressed in this volume.

1 The Semantics of Natural Language

The perspective on semantics taken in introductory logic courses can roughly be described as follows: In these contexts, the goal is to give a general account of specific semantic relationships, such as the validity of an argument (form). An argument is said to be valid if the truth of the premises guarantees the truth of the conclusion. It's often emphasized that such relationships are at least sometimes instantiated in virtue of the *logical form* of sentences and their constituents. An aspect of logic is then to judge how the logical form of sentences determines issues such as validity of arguments (or argument-forms).

In this context, several other properties regarding truth and meaning are discussed. One guiding idea is that in order to understand what it is for a simple sentence to be true, we should try to find the basic constituents of such sentences and assign objects (individuals, sets, or functions) as values to them, thus developing an extensional semantics. This will yield an idea of how to understand how a simple sentence acquires its truth value. In a next step, we can investigate the dependence relation holding between truth-values of *complex* sentences, which are built out of simple sentences and (specific) sentential operators, such as 'not', 'and', 'or', and 'if...then', and the truth-values of these simple sentences and the meaning of the sentential operators. Quantifiers, such as 'all' and 'some', are accommodated in this picture.

But what are the basic constituents of simple sentences? Nowadays, simple sentences like "John is a philosopher" are usually thought of as consisting of a *singular term*, 'John', and a *predicate*, 'is a philosopher'. But how does such a sentence's truth-value depend upon the semantic values of the sentence's constituents? The idea is that the semantic value of a predicate is the set of all and only those objects to which the predicate applies—that is: the predicate's extension. Similarly, the semantic value of a name or a singular term is regarded as the object it refers to. In our case, it is John. The sentence 'John is a philosopher' is true iff John belongs to the set of all philosophers (and if it is true/false, it is true/false *because* John belongs/does not belong to that set).

The guiding idea is that the meaning (and the truth) of a complex expression fully depends upon (i) its constituents' meanings and (ii) these constituents' arrangement. This principle is usually called the principle of *compositionality*. Now, this picture, according to which the semantic value of an n-place predicate is its extension (a set of n-tuples or, if n=1, of individuals), and according to which the semantic value of a singular term is its referent, faces a number of problems, three of which will be highlighted in the present context. The first is the problem of how to determine which semantic value a singular term contributes to the semantic content expressed by a sentence. Let us come back to the examples introduced above. If we compare the first two sentences, we are dealing with the difference between a *proper name* and a *definite description* (of the structure "the F", where "F" is a predicate):

(1) *John Perry* is a Stanford professor.

(2) *The philosopher the edition by Newen and van Riel is dedicated to* is a Stanford professor.

The difference between (1) and (2) can be accounted for by describing the difference between the contribution of "John Perry" and the contribution of "the philosopher the edition by Newen and van Riel is dedicated to" to the semantic content of the sentence. A standard view of definite descriptions holds that a(n attributively used) definite description's semantic content is characterized by the description itself, while the semantic content of a proper name is the object referred to. Thus, there is a standard semantic solution to the problem of the difference in the semantic contributions of proper names and definite descriptions. However, this alleged solution does not work in the case of proper names and indexicals (as well as referentially used definite descriptions). Let us compare the following sentences:

(1) *John Perry* is a professor at Stanford.
(1a) *He* (pointing to a person visible in the mirror) is a professor at Stanford.
(3) *I* am professor at Stanford. (Uttered by John Perry)

There are modal arguments which show that the semantic contribution of proper names and indexicals is the object referred to by the expression (in a given context). But the reference of the singular terms used in (1), (1a), and (3) is always the same. Therefore, the semantic content of the sentences, which is constituted by the semantic values of the components, should be the same. But as we have seen above, the cognitive dynamics of the contents expressed by the sentences are different. Let us illustrate this using the additional example of (1a) in contrast to (3). If John sees himself in a mirror, under certain conditions he may not recognize himself. He may think that the person he is seeing is not a professor at Stanford (because his jacket is too shabby), even though he believes that he himself is a Professor at Stanford. How can we deal with the difference in cognitive significance?

On the one hand, there is the Neo-Fregean view according to which we need to consider two components of semantic content; one component is the object referred to and the second component is a mode of presentation associated with the expression. Simplifying a bit, in this view, the mode of presentation associated with "I" can be characterized by the rule "the speaker of the utterance", while in the case of "he" it can be characterized by "the person the speaker is pointing to". This strategy allows us to distinguish the semantic value of the three sentences above, given that the mode of presentation can be interpreted as determining or being part of the semantic value. But the concept of a mode of presentation faces several problems; for example, sometimes, one has or possesses a number of different modes of presentation associated with one proper name, and one lacks a criterion to select which one is appropriate. Moreover, sometimes one seems to lack modes of presentation completely. In combination with the modal argument of Kripke (1980), this leads to a revival of the Neo-Russellian view according to which the semantic value of proper names and indexicals is always the object referred to: This claim is also called *the theory of direct reference for proper names and indexicals*. Most Neo-Russellians decided to rely on a difference between semantics and pragmatics to account for the differences in cognitive significance of the sentences (1), (1a), and (3), i.e. they claim that the epistemic difference is not a semantic one, but only a pragmatic one. In the context of this debate, Perry develops his own view, trying to keep the insights of both, the Fregean as well as the Russellian tradition.

Analogous problems show up when we are dealing with the respective attitude reports. The sentences (4) to (6) may differ in truth values, although we just have to substitute co-referential singular terms to receive one sentence from the others. We receive different truth-values given the epistemic background condition described above:

(4) John believes that John Perry is a professor at Stanford University.
(5) John believes that the philosopher this book is dedicated to is a professor at Stanford University.
(6) John believes that he himself is a professor at Stanford University.

How can we develop an adequate semantics for propositional attitude reports? Obviously, this question is intimately related to the question of the distinct cognitive roles the embedded sentences play. Accordingly, when dealing with the semantics of propositional attitude reports, one has to answer the question of whether the theory of direct reference is valid in all contexts. If an expression has the same meaning in all contexts, we speak of *semantic innocence*. Neo-Russellians start with the theory of direct reference for names and indexicals and most of them defend the idea of semantic innocence. But then we have the problem of how to deal with the fact that there is a difference in truth-values although the only difference between the sentences is the difference in singular terms. Perry, together with Crimmins (Perry 1989b), develops a view that gives up semantic innocence for names and indexicals. He argues that in attitude reports the semantic contribution of a singular term to the thought expressed by the report is not only the object referred to, but also a notion *n* which a thinker has in his mind; a notion includes a special way of thinking about the object as part of the thought ascribed by the report. So Perry gives up strict compositionality to develop a semantics of attitude reports on the basis of a theory of direct reference for names and indexicals. Concerning this debate, it is worth noting that the problem of propositional attitudes extends to the meaning of predicates. One might want to hold that two predicates that differ in meaning may designate or signify the same property; a standard example is the following: 'is an equiangular triangle' and 'is an equilateral triangle'. At least, these predicates have the same extension, and necessarily so. Nevertheless, one might believe that a given triangle is equiangular without thereby believing that it is equilateral.

Ideally, the different solutions to numerous specific semantic problems focusing on singular terms and on indexicals, especially focusing on the use of "I", need to be integrated in a general semantic framework. Such a framework was developed by Perry and Jon Barwise in their book "Situations and Attitudes" (1983B). This initiated a new line of semantics under the title *situation semantics*.

The main strategy Perry pursues when discussing these topics can also be characterized by contrasting it with (a somewhat idealized version of) the orthodox view in the philosophy of language. According to the orthodox view, the reference of singular terms and semantic issues in general should be worked out within a framework that dissociates persons, their minds, and intentions, on the one hand, and language, on the other, which somehow lives its own life beyond the mental life of individual speakers and their contexts. Perry adopts a different strategy: He tries to tie the functioning of language to the mental life of persons who use language and to their way of interacting with the world. According to him, it is *speakers* who refer to objects *using* singular terms in a context of actions, rather than singular terms (in a primary sense of 'referring'); it is mental aspects of speakers that ground different meanings of co-referential expressions, such as 'he' (uttered in an appropriate context) and 'the philosopher this volume is dedicated to'; and we should focus on speakers in contexts of language use in order to get an idea of how information is conveyed by language, how context-sensitivity really works, and how truth and meaning interrelate.

In the present volume, the first four chapters deal with Perry's work in the philosophy of language – three being concerned with specific issues and one being concerned with his overarching account of the semantics of natural language in general. The first three chapters, respectively, are on *indexicality* (written by Jérôme Dokic), the theory of direct reference and the meaning of singular terms (presented by Kepa Korta), and propositional attitudes (developed by Albert Newen). The fourth chapter is on the situation semantics that Perry developed with Jon Barwise (written by Isidora Stojanovic).

The second part of this book concerns aspects regarding the *self*, *persons*, and the *ontological foundations of mental phenomena*; notably,

Perry's work on these topics is deeply connected with his work in semantics.

2 Persons as Mental Beings

In this part, three aspects of Perry's work are discussed: his account of one of the most intriguing and distinctive features of selves, i.e. the capacity for self-knowledge (presented by Neil Van Leeuwen), his account of persons and personal identity, or what makes, say, the old man sitting in his chair the same as the boy in the picture taken more than half a century ago (written by Raphael van Riel), and his account of what kind of entity the mind is, i.e. his overarching metaphysical picture that situates minds within a naturalist ontology (discussed by Daniel Cohnitz). Again, let us give a rough idea of these topics.

Consider sentence (6) again:

(6) John believes that he himself is a professor at Stanford University.

First of all, it seems that John has this believe if and only if he has a belief, the content of which is expressed by the sentence "I am professor at Stanford University" when uttered by him. Now, interestingly, having this belief, John seems to be in a position *to know* that he has this belief and that this belief is about himself. He does not have to run an experiment, check his e-mails or ask a colleague—having this belief (explicitly) is sufficient for him to be in a position to know that he has this belief. This highlights one aspect of what is often referred to as *self-knowledge*. It should be noted that this epistemological issue is intimately connected to semantic issues as presented above.

But one may also have a belief about oneself *without noticing* that it is about oneself, as we have illustrated with the following sentence:

(5) John believes that the philosopher this book is dedicated to is a professor at Stanford University.

If John Perry were to believe that the philosopher this book is dedicated to is John Searle, who he knows works at Berkeley, he would evaluate (5) as false. The important aspect is that if he thinks of Searle by relying on the (attributively used) description "the philosopher this book is dedicated to", then he actually thinks about himself, though he is unaware of this. He is lacking the immediate self-representations which are involved in de se thoughts and which constitute a special way of thinking about oneself—a way that is connected to specific motivations to act: Only if John Perry thinks that *he himself* should go to the meeting now, he is disposed to hurry up. But if he thinks that the philosopher this book is dedicated to should go to the meeting now, he may just do nothing (or give John Searle a call). Thus, we have to characterize a special way of self-knowledge by introducing self-notions as mental entities.

Self-knowledge and self-representation, however, do not form the only pressing topics associated with persons and selves. The paradigmatic entities endowed with consciousness, beliefs, desires, and experiences are persons, and to many, being a person is a necessary condition for being a morally or legally responsible subject. Similarly, some would hold that to be free, one has to be a person. But what *are* persons? Or, put differently though still intuitively, what makes a person the person she is? Perry gave this question a specific interpretation, namely: What is it for two objects (called 'person-stages') to belong to the same person? What makes the entity writing this sentence and the entity that wrote the previous sentence a few seconds ago belong to the same person, namely, to me? Perry's basic idea is that to give an account of personal identity is to give a relation in virtue of which two (or more) person stages existing at different times belong to the same person. Building on his discussion of this topic in the writings of Locke, Hume, Butler, Reid and others, Perry defends the idea that this relation has to be interpreted as a *mental* relation. That is: An object existing at one time and an object existing at another time belong to the same person only if they instantiate a specific mental relation. This leads to the last aspect this volume tries to shed light on: Perry's work on the metaphysics of the mind.

What sort of entities are mental beings? Perry "antecedently" believes that mental beings are physical in nature, and that there are no phenomenal properties that do not belong to the set of physical properties. The strategy is not to decide the issue on independent grounds, but rather to see whether or not the physicalist can defend his or her position against the threat of dualism, i.e. the doctrine that there are more properties or entities than just the physical ones. Two influential lines of argument in favor of dualism have been presented in recent years—Frank Jackson's Mary-argument and Saul Kripke's modal argument. Let us just briefly introduce one of them to sketch Perry's reaction: In the Mary-argument, we are invited to conceive of a situation in which a person, Mary, knows all there is to know about (the relevant aspects of) perception that can be learned from the study of textbooks in a black-and-white room. Mary is, so to speak, a perfectly informed neuroscientist, but part of the experiences she learned about are such that she never lived through them—she never saw any colored objects. One day, she leaves the black-and-white room and is presented with a ripe tomato. It is only then, or so the argument goes, that she (in a sense) learns what it is like to see a red tomato. But then, there is information about vision not captured by neuroscience. The dimension that is seemingly not captured by neuroscience is referred to by the term 'qualia' (used to single out the quality of my experience). Qualia are, thus, properties that cannot be captured by neuroscience, or so the argument goes.

Roughly, Perry tries to draw a line between what is, intuitively speaking, the metaphysical level associated with this thought-experiment (i.e. the realm of properties, neural processes, and qualia) and the way these are made available to us. He argues that the argument is mistaken in that it draws conclusions about the metaphysical level from assumptions about the level at which things are presented to us: As an antecedent physicalist he holds, until shown to be wrong, that all mental phenomena are special physical phenomena, and on this basis, he argues that we can describe Mary's new knowledge when first seeing a tomato without being forced to accept dualism. Again, Perry builds upon his semantic framework in order to argue that the Mary-argument and the modal argument fail (the modal argument is not analogous to the Mary-argument—the main strategy Perry pursues in developing his counter-argument, however, is similar).

John Perry's work is not limited to the topics addressed in this volume. However, we hope that this volume provides a useful introduction to a number of central themes of the rich work of John Perry and, thereby, to a number of key issues in modern philosophy of mind and language.

Part One

Language

2

Indexicality

JÉRÔME DOKIC

1 Introduction

The phenomenon of indexicality has justly attracted many philosophers. It is both very concrete—as we shall see below, indexicality is first and foremost a property of linguistic expressions—and relevant to extremely difficult issues, including the Cogito, consciousness, materialism, self-knowledge, perspectival thought, and the nature of belief. An adequate treatment of indexicality, then, promises to shed light on perennial questions in the philosophy of language, mind, and nature. Along with David Kaplan, John Perry is a pioneer in the field of contemporary studies on indexicality, although of course there are important precursors (Perry himself mentions Charles Sanders Peirce, Arthur Burks, and Hector-Neri Castañeda, and we can add a few others, such as Karl Bühler). Kaplan's work is more formal, though, and Perry went much farther in the exploration of the foundations of our cognitive architecture. This is why his work is highly relevant not only to present-day philosophy but to cognitive science as a whole.[1]

2 What Is Indexicality?

The definition of the notion of indexicality is controversial. There is no consensus on its exact boundaries. However, everybody agrees that indexi-

[1] Space prevents me from discussing Perry's application of his theory of indexicality to issues such as the nature of phenomenal consciousness (see Perry 2001B1).

Identity, Language, and Mind: An Introduction to the Philosophy of John Perry.
Albert Newen and Raphael van Riel (eds.).

cality is at least the property of a specific class of *linguistic expressions*. The following (non-exhaustive) list is typical of what is considered by linguists and philosophers of language to be indexical expressions, or indexicals for short:

Personal pronouns: "I", "you", "he", "she", etc.
Demonstratives, simple and complex: "this", "that", "this man", "that woman", etc.[2]
Adverbs: "here", "now", "presently", "today", "yesterday".
Adjectives: "my", "your", "present".
Verb tenses: present tense, past tense, etc.

These expressions are called "indexical" insofar as their significance (to use a neutral phrase at this stage) can vary in systematic ways according to the context of their utterance. In short, indexicality has to do with a form of *context-sensitivity* that some linguistic expressions exhibit in contrast to others.[3]

In 1914, the logician and philosopher Gottlob Frege described the phenomenon of indexicality in the following way, by reference to the complex indexical "this man":

> Of course I can use the words "this man" to designate now this man, now that man. But still on each occasion I mean them to designate just one man. The sentences of our everyday language leave a good deal to guesswork. It is the surrounding circumstances that enable us to make the right guess. The sentence I utter does not always contain everything that is necessary; a great deal has to be supplied by the context, by the gestures I make and the direction of my eyes. But a language that is intended for scientific employment must not leave anything to guesswork. (Frege 1979: 213)

In this passage, Frege makes clear that he views indexicality as a property of *ordinary* language. From a logical point of view, indexicality is a

---

[2] The noun "demonstrative" is sometimes used as a synonym of "indexical", but more often demonstratives are taken to be a sub-class of indexicals, namely those that are accompanied by a *demonstration* (see Kaplan 1989a and b).

[3] Beyond the standard list of indexical expressions, some philosophers claim that indexicality is also hidden in other expressions, including names, natural kind terms, propositional attitudes verbs, and vague predicates. An extreme view, which we may call "panindexicalism", is that the very notion of a non-indexical sentence is empty. However, panindexicalism is likely to rest on the false presupposition that indexicality is the only form of context-sensitivity that language exhibits. See Perry's "Thought Without Representation" (1986d) for discussion of an important non-indexical form of context-sensitivity.

defect, and should be banned from artificial languages more suited to scientific use.[4]

Frege uses the notion of *designation* or *reference* (*Bedeutung*, in German) to capture that which can vary across contexts of utterance. In the context of a particular utterance, the complex demonstrative "this man" can refer to a particular man, but the very same expression can be used to refer to any other man. Intuitively at least, this demonstrative behaves in a quite different way from proper names, like "Peter" or "Mary", whose reference is much more stable across contexts of utterances, even if we take homonyms into account.

As a further illustration of the phenomenon of indexicality, consider the following dialogue:

(1) Mary: "I'm right, you're wrong."

Peter: "No, I'm right, you're wrong."

Mary and Peter use the very same type of sentence, individuated by syntax and vocabulary, but what they say in uttering this sentence is quite different. Mary says that she herself is right and Peter is wrong, while Peter says that he himself is right and Mary is wrong. This is why they have a genuine disagreement. So the indexicals "I" and "you" can hardly be assimilated to proper names, as they refer to different persons in different contexts of utterance.

Perry (2001B2: §3.4) says that in the case of indexicals, context is used *semantically*. Roughly, context is used semantically only if it needs to be consulted even after the language, words and linguistic meanings relevant to the interpretation of the utterance have already been determined. Consider the following exchange:

(2) Mary: "The bank is finally open."

Peter: "You are wrong: The bank is not open."

Suppose that Mary intends to refer to her financial institution, where she wants to make a withdrawal, whereas Peter has in mind the border of the river, which has been closed to pedestrians as the result of a recent flooding. Clearly, Mary and Peter talk at cross-purposes. They do not even *disagree*. They are simply misunderstanding each other. In such a case, Perry says

---

[4] This is not to say that Frege had nothing interesting to say about indexicality in ordinary language. In fact, he suggested at several places that context can play a *symbolic role*, in the sense that it can contribute to the *expression* of a determinate thought. For instance, an utterance of the sentence "It's over now" expresses a complete thought only along with the time of the utterance itself. This suggestion has been overlooked by both Kaplan's and Perry's discussions of Frege (see Künne 1992 and Mulligan and Smith 1986).

that context must be used *pre-semantically* in order to disambiguate the vocable "bank", which in fact corresponds to *two* different English words.

Indexicals do not work like that. In English at least, the vocable "I" corresponds to the same word, as it figures in any standard dictionary. Context is needed to determine what is said by an utterance involving "I" (which person is referred to), but only after the word itself has been properly identified as the first-person pronoun.

Perry also contrasts the case of indexicals with what he calls "post-semantic" or "content-supplemental" ways of using context. Consider this dialogue:

(3) Mary: It's raining.

Peter: No, it's not raining.

Do Mary and Peter have a genuine disagreement? Well, it depends on the situation. If their utterances both concern the same place, they disagree. On the other hand, if they talk over the phone from different cities so that Mary's utterance concerns London, while Peter's utterance concerns Paris, they do not really disagree; perhaps they are both right. In order to know what Mary and Peter say, we have to look at the broader context of their utterances and determine a relevant place. As Perry puts it, we have to make a content-supplemental use of context.

Why is the latter example a case of *post*-semantic use of context? Well, the sentence "It's raining" does not involve any indication as to the relevant place where it is supposed to rain. As interpreters, we have to exploit other aspects of the context of utterance. In contrast, the indexical sentence "It's raining here" *does* involve an indication as to a relevant place. As Perry puts it, indexicals have linguistic meanings that "direct" us to certain aspects of the context; in the case in point, where the speaker is located. However, the sort of meaning indexicals have is a difficult issue, to which we now turn.

3 Divide and Conquer?

Perry does not share Frege's view that indexicality is a mere inconvenience of ordinary language. On the contrary, he has shown it to constitute a serious challenge to Frege's conception of language and its significance. More specifically, Perry argues in "Frege on Demonstratives" (1977) that Frege's notion of sense is either inconsistent or leads to insuperable problems.

In Frege's system, any (simple or complex) significant part of language has a reference. For the sake of simplicity, we can draw a distinction between singular terms, which refer to objects (individuals), and general terms, which refer to properties. Now Frege insisted that any referring expression is related to the world by way of its sense (*Sinn* in German). The sense of an expression involves a specific way in which the reference is given, what we now call a "mode of presentation" of the reference.[5] On the one hand, the sense of an expression *determines* the expression's reference, so that a given sense cannot determine more than one reference. On the other hand, two expressions can have the same reference but different senses. A sense leads us to a unique reference but, as Russell once put it, there is no road back from reference to sense. Frege's most famous example involves the expressions "the Morning Star" and "the Evening Star", which both refer to the planet Venus by way of different senses or modes of presentation.

Frege applied the tripartite distinction word/sense/reference to both singular and general terms. In a famous letter to Husserl dated May 24, 1891, he offers the following summary of his view of language:[6]

Table 2.1

	sentence	**singular term**	**general term** (= concept-word)
sense (*Sinn*)	thought (*Gedanke*)	sense of the singular term	sense of the general term
reference (*Bedeutung*)	truth-value	object	concept[7]

In "On Sense and Reference", Frege introduced the notion of sense to deal with epistemological problems involving identity sentences. Frege observed that a true identity statement can be *a posteriori*, in the sense that it can convey a substantial piece of information to the rational man. This is puzzling, for after all, what is said by a true identity statement is just that an object is identical with itself, which is hardly informative. For instance, the French writer Romain Gary wrote novels under the pseudonym "Émile Ajar", so that it is true that Romain Gary is Émile Ajar. We now know that

---

[5] The German phrase used by Frege is "Art des Gegebenseins", which literally means "way of being given". In the context of contemporary discussions of Frege, senses and modes of presentation are often considered as the same. However, Frege made clear (at the beginning of "On Sense and Reference" [1892]) that senses *involve* or *contain* modes of presentation of the references. It is not clear that this distinction is of any relevance to Perry's criticism of Frege.

[6] Table 2.1 is a variation on Frege's own diagram, which is reproduced in Frege 1976.

[7] Frege's use of the term "concept" (*Begriff*) is notoriously non-standard. What most contemporary philosophers call "concepts" correspond to the senses of general terms or predicates, rather than their references. Fregean concepts are extensional entities, namely functions from objects to truth-values.

this is true, but the committee of the Prix Goncourt in France did not possess the relevant information when they unknowingly gave the prize twice to the same writer.

It is not entirely clear how Frege actually solved the problem of informative true identity statements, but he certainly thought that his notion of sense could do the trick. The names "Romain Gary" and "Émile Ajar" are co-referential (in the relevant context of use), but they express different senses, and the fact that theses senses determine the same reference is not something that can be known *a priori*, i.e. by merely understanding the names or, as Frege put it, by grasping their respective senses.

Perry realized that Frege was trying to put his notion of sense to two theoretical roles that are at least *prima facie* quite different. On the one hand, the sense of an expression plays a *semantic* role; it determines the reference. As Perry observes (1993B: 5), this generates a criterion of difference for thoughts, conceived as the senses of complete (true or false) sentences:

> *Frege's Semantic Criterion*: If sentence S is true and sentence S' is not, S and S' must express different thoughts.

Two sentences can have the same truth-value while expressing different thoughts (i.e. having different senses), like "Socrates is a philosopher" and "Grass is green", which are both true. However, two sentences that have different truth-values must express different thoughts. For instance, "Grass is green" and "Grass is blue" cannot have the same sense, since one is true but the other is false.

On the other hand, the sense of an expression plays an *epistemic* role; it is supposed to capture what the subject knows when she understands the expression. This yields another criterion of difference for thoughts:[8]

> *Frege's Epistemic Criterion*: If subject A is rational, understands both S and S', and accepts S as true without accepting S' as true (at the same time), S and S' must express different thoughts.[9]

The gist of Perry's criticism of Frege is that nothing can play both a semantic and an epistemic role. Perry's positive contribution is to split Fregean senses into two distinct theoretical entities.

---

[8] In "Frege on Demonstratives", Perry introduces a third criterion of difference, which is connected to Frege's doctrine that the reference of expression in so-called "indirect contexts" is their ordinary sense, but for the sake of simplicity I shall leave this criterion aside here.

[9] The qualification "at the same time" is needed to exclude cases in which the subject *changes her mind* between the time at which she accepts S as true and the time at which she accepts S' as true. For if we do not exclude such cases, the criterion could posit differences in thought content where there are none.

In colloquial English, we may say that a descriptive thought can be "about" an object in the world. For instance, the thought expressed by the sentence "The shortest man on earth is bald" is about a particular person, namely the shortest man on earth (assuming that there is one; see below). The object of the descriptive thought is the entity, whatever it is, that satisfies the definite description "the shortest man on earth". The thought is true if that man is bald; it is false otherwise. So we have a general model of how a thought can be about an object. The thought is associated with a condition (e.g. being the shortest man on earth) and the thought's object is whatever meets the condition.

Notably, Frege himself balked at such a model. To begin with, when we entertain a thought about some object, there is a sense in which we have that object "in mind", as we say. However, it is not clear that we have in mind a particular person, say an inhabitant of an inaccessible valley in Sumatra, when we entertain the thought that the shortest man on earth is bald. The problem here is that our thought does not seem to be intrinsically, indeed magically related to any particular person. The epistemic relation between a descriptive thought and its "object" is at best indirect, in the sense that the thought's content is not affected by whether there is anything meeting the relevant condition. Perhaps there is no shortest man on earth, because at least two men happen to have exactly the same size. This would not deprive us from the possibility of entertaining the thought that the shortest man on earth is bald, although it is not clear whether our thought is false or rather neither true nor false. In Frege's own terms, the sense of the definite description "the shortest man on earth" does not seem to determine a particular reference.

Still, the model of descriptive thought remains quite powerful when we think about how our thoughts are related to their objects. First, Frege himself did not really give any substantial alternative account of what sense is. The thesis that sense determines reference is really nothing but a formal constraint on such an account; it merely forbids the assignment of more than one reference to any given sense.

Second, one might raise the question of whether demonstrative thoughts belong to the class of descriptive thoughts. This is a question that Perry carefully examines in "Frege on Demonstratives". Suppose that Leo utters the following sentence, involving the first-person indexical "I":

(4) I am rich.

In uttering this sentence, Leo entertains the demonstrative thought that he himself is rich. Now the suggestion is that the thought grasped by Leo is identical with the thought expressed by a descriptive thought of the following form:

(5) The D is rich.

In (5), "the D" is a definite description. The suggestion is then that Leo thinks about a more or less specific condition D that he applies to himself when he uses the first-person pronoun "I".

As Perry observes, this suggestion faces serious problems.[10] First, a rational subject can use the indexical "I" to talk and think about himself without possessing any definite self-description. For instance, Leo might be an amnesic in a sensory deprivation tank, and literally not know anything about his biography or current environment. He might rationally accept (4) while remaining agnostic about (5). Thus, by Frege's Epistemic Criterion, the thoughts expressed by (4) and (5) cannot be identical.

Second, even if Leo uses some self-description, there is no guarantee that he actually satisfies the description. For instance, poor Leo might think of himself as the tallest man on earth, while in fact wealthy Pierre is such a person. If "the D" in (5) is "the tallest man on earth", (5) is true while (4) is false. Thus, by Frege's Semantic Criterion, the thoughts expressed by (4) and (5) cannot be identical.

Of course, these problems generalize. For any condition D, we can construe cases in which the subject accepts (4) but not (5), and/or cases in which (4) and (5) have different truth-values. By Frege's own criteria, no sentence of the form "The D is rich" (at least when "the D" does not involve indexicals) can express the same thought as the thought expressed by Leo when he utters (4). It follows that we do not know what completes the predicative sense expressed by "__ is rich" in (4). In Perry's terms, we do not know what the completing senses expressed by indexicals are. Nothing seems to fit Frege's bill.

4 Linguistic Meanings and Psychological Roles?

Even though indexical expressions can refer to different things from one utterance to another, they seem to have a *stable linguistic meaning*. There are not several dictionary entries for a given indexical, corresponding to each possible reference that the indexical can have in some context of utterance. For instance, when someone we meet for the first time introduces herself with the words "I am Angelina", we understand what she is saying, although the indexical "I" as uttered in this context has (for us) a new reference.

---

10 At this point, Perry acknowledges his debt to Castañeda's seminal work, which dates back to the 1960's. Many of Castañeda's insights can be found in his later book (Castañeda 1989).

In fact, the linguistic meaning of indexicals can often be specified in the form of a unique *rule of reference*, which quantifies over contexts of utterance:

> Any utterance of "I" refers to the speaker of the utterance.
> Any utterance of "now" refers to the time of utterance.
> Any utterance of "here" refers to the place of utterance.
> Any utterance of "today" refers to the day of utterance.
> Etc.

Linguistic meanings are very different from Fregean senses. The linguistic meaning of an indexical does not determine its reference absolutely, but only relative to a context of utterance. Slightly more formally, it can be modeled as a function from contexts of utterances to references: persons, times, places, etc.[11] Depending on the context of utterance, the very same function can yield different values. For instance, when Hume and Heimson (who holds the delusive belief that he is David Hume; see Perry 1977) both utter the sentence "I wrote the 'Treatise'", they follow the same rule of reference, but refer to two distinct persons, and of course only one is right.

A philosopher sympathetic to the Fregean framework can welcome linguistic meanings along with senses and references. However, Perry makes the following suggestion, which constitutes a fairly important departure from Frege. According to Perry, the linguistic meaning of an indexical is the key to the individuation or classification of our psychological states. More precisely, it helps us to determine whether two token thoughts belong to the same psychological type. On this view, two English speakers uttering the same indexical sentence "I am rich" thereby express the same psychological state, although of course they say different things (one utterance might be true and the other false). If the speakers believe what they say, their utterances result from the same belief state.[12]

What is Perry's argument for the claim that indexical thoughts should be classified by means of context-invariant linguistic meanings? In general, thoughts are ascribed to subjects in the context of psychological explanations, including explanations of the subject's behavior. For instance, if Peter is thirsty and believes that there is something in the fridge that will quench his thirst, we expect him (*ceteris paribus*, as philosophers say, i.e. given

[11] In this respect, linguistic meanings are akin to what David Kaplan calls "characters".

[12] Using the terminology introduced in "Belief and Acceptance" (1980a), the speakers *accept* the same sentence. In general, one believes something *by* accepting a sentence. In this essay, Perry makes clear that even non-linguistic animals can have beliefs by accepting sentences in his sense, even though they cannot express the latter. Similarly, the fact that we theorists classify thoughts with the help of linguistic meanings does not entail that the subjects of these thoughts do possess the faculty of language.

assumptions about Peter's other propositional attitudes) to walk to the fridge and look there for something to drink. Now Perry observes that two speakers, say Peter and Mary, uttering the sentence "I'm about to be attacked by a bear" might *behave in the same way* (*ceteris paribus*), even though the thoughts they express are different. Indeed, these thoughts are not truth-conditionally equivalent (they are not true in the same conditions), since one is about Peter while the other is about Mary. Given the assumption that Peter and Mary are cognitively alike in other respects (for instance, neither is suicidal), the fact that they both think the same (type of) indexical thought, expressed by the sentence "I'm about to be attacked by a bear", explains the similarity in their behavior.

Perry's claim that indexical sentences should be used to individuate or classify the corresponding psychological states does not entail that we generally think of things under the descriptions provided by the corresponding rules of reference. For instance, when Peter thinks the thought expressed by his utterance of "I am thirsty", he probably does not think of himself as the speaker of this utterance. Indeed, in extraordinary circumstances, he might not even believe that he himself is the speaker of what is in fact his own utterance. It is not very plausible either that Peter thinks of himself as the speaker of a particular *thought*, namely the very thought that occupies his current thinking. This would entail that sophisticated concepts such as the concept of a particular thought are involved whenever one uses the first-person pronoun, or thinks about oneself.

On Perry's more recent view (see Perry 1990c, 2001B2), what correspond to indexicals in our minds are what he calls "notions", namely mental representations of particular entities. These notions are mental files having specific epistemic and pragmatic roles. For instance, what corresponds to the indexical "I" at the level of thought is a *self-notion*, which contains information the subject gets in "normally self-informative ways" (including proprioception, e.g., I feel a tension in my left leg), and motivates actions that are "normally self-effective" (e.g., I immediately stretch my left leg). I cannot feel a tension in somebody else's leg, and I can only move immediately my own leg. Of course my self-notion also contains information (or misinformation) about myself that I have acquired in other ways, such as by reading my birth certificate.

5 The Varieties of Indexicals

For the sake of simplicity, I assumed in the previous section that there is a one-to-one correspondence between indexical sentences, individuated in terms of their linguistic meanings, and the psychological profiles of the thoughts expressed by these sentences in each context of utterance. Even if this assumption is arguably true in some cases (such as those involving the indexical "I"), it cannot be maintained in full generality. The problem is that in other cases, the linguistic meaning of the indexical does not fully determine the cognitive significance of the corresponding thought-element. Suppose that Peter is seeing what, unbeknownst to him, is the stern and the bow of the same ship, whose middle is occluded by a big wall. He can intelligibly say something like "This ship [pointing to the stern] is not the same as this ship [pointing to the bow]". Of course, what he says is false, but it is so only *a posteriori*. So the thought-constituents expressed by the two occurrences of "this ship" cannot have the same cognitive significance (see Wettstein 1986).

To handle such cases, in which linguistic meaning does not fully determine cognitive significance, Perry (2001B2: 59) proposes the following taxonomy of indexical expressions (slightly simplified here):

Table 2.2

	Narrow context	**Wide context**
Automatic	I, now*, here*, today	Yea
Discretionary	now, here	that, this man, there, he, she

The context exploited by an indexical is *narrow* if it includes only the agent, time, and position of the utterance. Otherwise, it is *wide*. For instance, an utterance of "It is yea big" exploits a sample of the relevant size as provided by the outstretched hands of the speaker. In order to understand what is said by this utterance, the audience has to *perceive* what the speaker is demonstrating.

The distinction between automatic and discretionary indexicals has to do with the absence or presence of low-level intentions on the speaker's part. Suppose that, around midnight, Pierre says "Today is your birthday", while being unsure whether the time is just before or just after. His utterance is still true or false depending on whether midnight has actually passed. Pierre's intentions seem irrelevant to determine the reference of "today" in this context. In contrast, something like a *directing intention* (Kaplan 1989b) is needed in order to determine the reference of an utterance of "This ship is impressive". Indexicals such as "now" and "here" can have automatic uses, but most often they are discretionary, since the extent of space or time to which they can be used to refer has almost no limit; think of "The dinosaurs are now extinct".

The first-person pronoun seems to be a paradigmatic case of an automatic indexical (an utterance involving "I" refers to the speaker of the utterance), but some philosophers (such as Karl Bühler) have argued that it can refer to different stretches of the speaker's life according to the context (see Bühler 1934). I can refer to myself narrowly, to my temporary self, or more widely, to my stable self as it has been for many years. If something like this difference makes sense, then "I" is a discretionary indexical after all.

The fact that linguistic meaning often underdetermines the psychological types to which our thoughts belong leads to a distinction between linguistic and psychological modes of presentation. Consider the following proposal, adapted from Recanati (1993):

Table 2.3

Level of utterance		Level of thought
linguistic meaning (linguistic mode of presentation) *vs* proposition expressed	=	objective/referential content *vs* cognitive content (psychological mode of presentation)

According to Recanati's proposal, the distinction between linguistic and psychological modes of presentation should be maintained even when the former fully determines the latter. For instance, an utterance of the sentence "I'm tired" can express the very same referential content as the thought that I am tired. However, the utterance involves a linguistic mode of presentation, which can be specified by the rule according to which an utterance of "I" refers to the speaker of the utterance. The thought expressed by the utterance does not involve any linguistic mode of presentation (I do not have to think of myself as the speaker of the utterance), but rather a psychological mode of presentation (which in the case in point Recanati calls **EGO**).

The distinction between linguistic and psychological modes of presentation does not affect Perry's criticism of Frege. Psychological modes of presentation cannot be equated with Fregean senses. The same psychological mode of presentation can determine more than one reference depending on the context. On Perry's view, our thoughts can be classified by means of context-invariant psychological modes of presentation, although their referential or objective contents are apt to change across contexts of (real or potential) utterances.

6 Essential Indexicality

In "The Problem of the Essential Indexical," Perry puts forward a claim about the role of indexical beliefs in the explanation of action. There are changes in behaviour, Perry argues, that can only be explained by beliefs whose expression involves indexical terms like "I", "now", "here", and "this". As Perry puts it, replacement of them by other terms "destroys the force of the explanation" (1993B: 35). Here is a now famous illustration of this claim with respect to the first-person pronoun:

> I once followed a trail of sugar on a supermarket floor, pushing my cart down the aisle on one side of a tall counter and back the aisle on the other, seeking the shopper with the torn sack to tell him he was making a mess. With each trip around the counter, the trail became thicker. But I seemed unable to catch up. Finally, it dawned on me. I was the shopper I was trying to catch. (Perry 1993B: 33)

Surely, the change in the shopper's behavior, namely stopping the cart instead of following the trail, is the result of some Gestalt switch in his thought ("Finally, it dawned on me"). What is the nature of this switch? Well, the shopper suddenly realizes that he himself is making a mess. In other words, he forms an indexical belief he could express with the sentence "I am making a mess".[13] Why is this belief essentially indexical, relative to the explanation of the shopper's change in behaviour? We can suppose that when the shopper was following the trail, he already had a belief about a man, namely John Perry, who was making a mess. Perhaps he pointed to a man in the mirror and did not realize that that man was in fact himself. So he formed a true belief he could express with the sentence "That man is making a mess". However, he failed to move from that belief to the belief that he himself is making a mess. Both beliefs have the same truth-conditions, in the sense that they are about the same objective state of affairs, but only the latter belief reflects the shopper's Gestalt switch. Thus, the presence of the first-person indexical is essential to the explanation of the shopper's change in behavior.

---

[13] Presumably, at least in Perry's example, the shopper literally changed his mind, since before the Gestalt switch he believed something he could express with "I am *not* making a mess".

Analogous examples involving other types of indexicals can easily be designed. For instance, even if I know that the meeting starts at 2 p.m., I may not rush when the time comes, because I may not know that it is 2 p.m. *now*. The indexical "now", or at least the psychological mode of presentation corresponding to it, seems to be essential to my decision to rush. Similarly, if I know that the meeting takes place in Salle des Actes, and I am in Salle des Actes, I may not sit down, because I may not know that Salle des Actes is *here*. The indexical "here", or the psychological mode of presentation corresponding to it, seems to be essential to my decision to stay and sit in the room.

Perry calls "locating beliefs" (1993B: 35) the beliefs about where one is, when it is, and who one is, which are decisive in shaping one's everyday behavior. The claim of the essential indexical is that these beliefs are essentially indexical. They must be beliefs whose canonical expression requires the use of some indexical, as in the sentences "Here is the Salle des Actes", "It's 2 p.m. now", or "I am John Perry".

Clearly, Perry's aim in "The Problem of the Essential Indexical" is not just to point out the existence of actions (or action tendencies, since analogous examples can be given with emotions) whose explanation requires indexical beliefs. His main claim is more ambitious, and concerns the essential role of indexicality in *mediating* one's conceptual thought and action. As Millikan puts it, "[t]he ability of an agent to project knowledge of the world into relevant action in the world depends on the ability to think indexical thoughts" (1993B: 265).[14] Indeed, Perry's point is that one's knowledge that the meeting starts at 2 p.m. in the Salle des Actes cannot project directly into action. It can project into action only in concert with indexical knowledge (or belief) to the effect that the meeting starts *hic et nunc*.

Perry argues that the Fregean framework is unable to explain why indexicality is essential. The difficulty is that "having a self-locating belief does not consist in believing a Fregean thought" (1993B: 21). Fregean thoughts are classical propositions, in the sense that they are true or false absolutely (not relative to any parameter, other than a possible world). However:

---

[14] In fact, Millikan is skeptical about the claim of the essential indexical. For instance, she argues that what corresponds to the indexical "I" in our minds is a non-indexical mental *proper name*, which *can* project directly into action. Millikan assumes that at the level of thought, the special symbol one uses to designate oneself as oneself is not context-sensitive, since its reference is always the same, namely oneself. This assumption has been challenged by Gordon (1995), who suggests that imagining being someone else might involve a use of the mental indexical "I" to refer to another person.

> The sentence "I am making a mess" does not identify a proposition. For this sentence is not true or false absolutely, but only as said by one person or another; had another shopper said it when I did, he would have been wrong. So the sentence by which I identify what I came to believe does not identify, by itself, a proposition. There is a missing conceptual ingredient: a sense for which I am the reference, or a complex of properties I alone have, or a singular term that refers to no one but me. (Perry 1993B: 37)

Perry doubts that the missing conceptual ingredient can be found. As we have seen above, I may not have any definite description that I could substitute for the first person pronoun, and even if I had one, it might not be true of myself, so that it might fail to target the appropriate reference. Analogous remarks apply to the other types of indexicals. More generally, what Perry calls "the doctrine of propositions", according to which beliefs can be fully analysed as relations to propositions, cannot be maintained.

7 The Reflexive-Referential Theory

Much of Perry's early work on indexicality is a sustained attempt to show that an adequate account of the phenomenon of indexicality forces us to split up the notion of Fregean sense into two distinct semantic properties: the linguistic meanings of indexical sentences, considered as properties of expression types, and the Russellian propositions or referential contents expressed by utterances of these sentences.[15] On the one hand, linguistic meanings reflect the projectible roles that belief states play in our cognitive economy, which is why we can appeal to them in order to explain human behavior. On the other hand, Russellian propositions typically capture what is said by utterances.

Perry's later work integrates indexicality in a much wider context. For the last decade he has been developing an ambitious theory of communication in which indexicality comes out as a special case of a more general phenomenon. The most salient change is that the older two-tiered approach gives way to a multitiered approach in which a given utterance or thought is associated with many levels of truth-conditions and contents. More precisely, utterances express various kinds of what Perry calls "reflexive contents" along with their referential or "official" contents.

Let us describe the basic tenets of Perry's reflexive-referential theory. Utterances and thoughts, considered as (respectively physical and mental)

---

[15] Russellian propositions (see Russell 1918) are propositions whose constituents are worldly objects and properties, rather than modes of presentation. For instance, the proposition expressed by "Mont-Blanc is more than 4000 meters high" is constituted by Mont-Blanc itself, along with the property of being more than 4000 meters high.

particulars, are true in certain conditions and false in others. Traditional truth-conditional semantics uses the following schematic biconditional to capture the truth-conditions of a given utterance *u*, where "iff" is the standard abbreviation for "if and only if":

(6) *u* is true iff *p*.

A potentially misleading feature of this simple schema is that it has an indefinite number of true instances, even when the utterance is fixed. For instance, the shopper's utterance *u* of the sentence "I am making a mess" is true iff the speaker of *u* is making of mess, but (as things are) it is also true iff John Perry is making a mess. It appears that one cannot speak of *the* truth-conditions of this utterance, since many propositions *p* can figure at the right-hand side of the relevant biconditional instance.

Now the reflexive-referential theory suggests a more perspicuous method for specifying the truth-conditions of utterances (and thoughts). According to this method, the biconditionals used to capture truth-conditions have the following form:

(7) Given constraints *c*, *u* is true iff *p*.

The proposition that *p* is the content of the utterance *u relative* to the constraints *c*. Among these constraints are the conventions of English and what Perry calls "connecting facts", such as the contingent fact that the speaker of the utterance is John Perry.

So the idea is that the same utterance or thought can be associated with different levels of truth-conditions depending on what is presupposed about the situation in question. Let us see how this new idea works with respect to a particular case. Suppose that Pierre utters the indexical sentence *s* "The meeting starts now". The truth-conditions of Pierre's utterance u_P can be specified in many different ways, including the following:

(8) Given facts about the linguistic meaning of *s*, u_P is true iff the meeting starts at the time of u_P.

Note that the proposition expressed by the right-hand side of this biconditional is *reflexive*, in the sense that it refers to the utterance itself. The notion of reflexive proposition or content is connected to the earlier notion of psychological role, but only indirectly. Competent speakers of English will know (at least tacitly) that any utterance of the English sentence "The meeting starts now" will be true iff the meeting starts at the time of the utterance. What they know are the reflexive *truth-conditions* of the sentence. Reflexive truth-conditions are what correspond to roles, meanings, or characters. Now it is only when these general conditions are *applied* to particular utterances, such as Pierre's, that we get their reflexive contents, such as the right-hand side of the biconditional in (8).

Reflexive content is also what the competent speaker of English knows about an utterance when she does not know when, where, and by whom the utterance has been produced. To give another oft-cited example of Perry (see 1993B: 134), suppose that you receive a postcard but are unable to read the timestamp or the signature. All that you can read is "I am having a good time here". Even if you do not know what the author of the postcard said in writing this sentence, you know at least that he or she was having a good time then, i.e. at the time the postcard was written.

Perry makes clear that the reflexive content specified by (8) does not usually correspond to what is said or what is believed by Pierre. Rather, what is said is the referential content of Pierre's utterance, which can be specified by fixing further facts about Pierre's situation:[16]

(9) Given facts about the linguistic meaning of *s*, and the fact that the time of u_P is 2 p.m., u_P is true iff the meeting starts at 2 p.m.

In contrast to (8), the proposition expressed by the right-hand side of the biconditional is *not* reflexive, since it does not involve the utterance itself as a constituent. It is called "referential" since it involves only the conditions that are put on the *subject matter* of Pierre's utterance, once we have fixed all the facts that determine reference. Perry also calls this content "official", since it corresponds to the notion of semantic content used by proponents of the direct theory of reference (among others, Ruth Barcan Marcus, Saul Kripke, Keith Donnellan, David Kaplan, and Howard Wettstein). In particular, referential content captures the modal profile of the utterance. For instance, even if all utterances of the sentence "I am here now" are true, what is said by their authors is not a necessary truth. It is a contingent fact that one is located at a given place at a given time.

The reflexive-referential theory is much more flexible that the earlier, two-tiered theory since it allows the semanticist to exploit several levels of truth-conditions and contents depending on her explanatory goals. Another advantage of the theory is that indexicality comes out as a special case of reflexivity, which concerns non-indexical expressions as well. Suppose for instance that *u* is my utterance of the sentence "Eros is trilingual". Even though "Eros" is not an indexical but a proper name, *u* has both reflexive and referential truth-conditions, as specified respectively in (10) and (11):

---

[16] Referential content is also called "incremental content" in Perry's "Individuals in Informational and Intentional Content" (1990b).

(10) Given facts about linguistic meaning, *u* is true iff the person one may designate with "Eros" in the convention *u* exploits is trilingual.

(11) Given facts about linguistic meaning plus the fact that the person one may designate with "Eros" in the convention *u* exploits is Eros Corazza, *u* is true iff Eros Corazza is trilingual.

Even is the hearer of *u* does not know that "Eros" designates Eros Corazza, the famous expert on indexicality, she can recover at least the reflexive truth-conditions of *u* as stated in (10). Note that linguistic meaning plays a quite different role in the case of indexicals and names. Indexicals are tied by their linguistic meanings to different relationships to the utterance, such as being its speaker or producer (in the case of "I"). In contrast, the linguistic meaning of names at best narrows down the set of permissive conventions exploited by the utterance. Since many persons may be called "Eros", which convention is actually at play cannot be determined merely at the level of meaning.

8 Less Is More: Radical Minimalism

The reflexive-referential theory is also more flexible than most versions of the orthodox theory of direct reference. In particular, the latter theory makes two assumptions that Perry both rejects.

(A1) What is said by an utterance is always its referential content.

(A2) The semantic content of an utterance is always its referential content.

Against the first assumption, Perry occasionally allows for what is said to diverge from referential content. Suppose for instance that Perry introduces himself to a stranger by uttering the sentence "I am John Perry". The referential content of Perry's utterance is as trivial and necessary as the proposition that John Perry is John Perry. But surely the stranger learns something interesting when John Perry said to him "I am John Perry". On the reflexive-referential theory, she learns that a certain reflexive proposition is true, namely that the speaker of this utterance is John Perry (or more precisely that one may call the speaker of this utterance "John Perry"). In this context, it is best to construe what is said as being determined by the reflexive content of the utterance rather than its referential content.

Someone can reject the first assumption and still adhere to the second one. For instance, one might think that semantics is primarily concerned with the determination of referential content, and that what is said by an utterance is a pragmatic matter (this is the view of Cappelen and Lepore

[2005]). In rejecting A2, Perry defends a quite different conception of the interface between semantics and pragmatics. On his view, recently developed in concert with Kepa Korta, the semantic content of an utterance is its *reflexive content*, given the meaning of the uttered sentence. This view might seem to give more justice to the intuitions that semantics has to do with general knowledge of language, while pragmatics concerns idiosyncratic features of the context of utterance, including speakers' intentions. As Perry says "semantics can give us *utterance-bound descriptions* of what is said, but cannot usually provide *utterance-free* descriptions of what is said" (2007c: 534). In other words, semantics is concerned with reflexive contents and not with referential contents. Reflexive contents are what we need to construct a truth-conditional and compositional theory of meaning.

In this respect, Perry and Korta's view about the natural dividing point between semantics and pragmatics is more minimalist than Cappelen and Lepore (2005)'s self-proclaimed semantic minimalism. Cappelen and Lepore argued that semantics proper is concerned with the resolution of the reference of indexical expressions, but should stop there. Perry and Korta deplore that we have already gone too far:

> What Kepa Korta and I propose is that the reflexive content, with meaning fixed, be taken as the semantic content … for [the] purposes [of] constructing a compositional, truth conditional theory of meaning. On the issue of ''pragmatic intrusion'' into semantic content, then, I am more radical, more minimal, than those, like Cappelen and Lepore (2005), who factor in contextually determined values for indexicals, and a number of other things (resolution of reference for demonstratives and names, resolution of ambiguity and vagueness) that, as far as I can see, would have to be based on speaker's intentions. (Perry 2007c: 529)

On their view, the semanticist is not particularly interested in the fact that John Perry is the referent of "I" in the context of the shopper's utterance of "I am making a mess". What she is interested in is the fact that this utterance is true iff the speaker is making a mess, whoever he or she is. The rest is only pragmatics, where referential content still plays an important role.

3

Holmes, Perry, and Reference

KEPA KORTA

I am bound to say that in all the accounts which you have been so good as to give of my own small achievements you have habitually underrated your own abilities. It may be that you are not yourself luminous, but you are a conductor of light. Some people without possessing genius have a remarkable power of stimulating it. I confess, my dear fellow, that I am very much in your debt.
[Sherlock Holmes to Dr. Watson]
Sir Arthur Conan Doyle, *The Hound of the Baskervilles*, Chapter 1.

1 Introduction

Dr. Watson admits that these words gave him "keen pleasure" for he "had often been piqued by his [Holmes's] indifference" to his admiration and to the efforts he had made to let the public know about Holmes's methods and achievements. According to Watson, Holmes "had never said as much", so he had good reason to get keen pleasure from those words. He doesn't tell, though, how he took Holmes's assessment of his attempt to apply the detective's methods:

> I am afraid, my dear Watson, that most of your conclusions were erroneous. When I said that you stimulated me I meant, to be frank, that in noting your fallacies I was occasionally guided towards the truth. (Ibid.)

After some years collaborating with John Perry, I wouldn't mind if it turned out that I had played Watson's role and stimulated and guided John towards the truth, just by producing, and showing him, the fallacious reasoning he shouldn't follow.

Identity, Language, and Mind: An Introduction to the Philosophy of John Perry.
Albert Newen and Raphael van Riel (eds.).

The Holmes and Watson analogy can well illustrate many aspects of my collaboration with Perry. He is a philosophical genius, a luminous mind; I'm not. His findings might not seem obvious, *prima facie*. But it's certainly very difficult not to be convinced by the simplicity and clarity of his arguments, which make you wonder, 'How did I not think of that myself?'

On the other hand, Perry, unlike Holmes, does write about his findings and methods, so there is no need for a Watson here. But there might be no harm if I play one; in giving my version of Perry's findings, I might again incur fallacies that help Perry and others to avoid some ways of reasoning they shouldn't follow.

I've been commissioned to do a presentation of John Perry's views on reference here. We may have a little problem, though. Due to my work with Perry on pragmatics during the last decade (Korta and Perry 2006c, 2008, 2009, 2011B), I'm not sure I can distinguish my own thinking from Perry's thinking on the matter. But the Holmes-Watson case may be helpful again. Once he knows about Holmes's view on any subject under investigation, Watson has no separate thoughts of his own; hence, all interesting findings he tells about cannot be his, but Holmes's. Nobody would think otherwise. Just apply the same principle here.

I'll start, in §2, by presenting what I think constitutes Perry's overall pragmatic picture on reference: Referring to things is not something that words do, but something that people do using words, and sometimes even without using words. The last point gives rise to one of the most debated issues in the recent philosophy of language: the issue of unarticulated constituents, an idea that Perry introduces when discussing the content of some of our thoughts in "Thought without Representation" (Perry 1986d). This article is widely interpreted as advocating a thesis about reference without words. I'll discuss his view, so interpreted, at the end of the chapter in §7. But first, in §3, I'll try to locate the origins of Perry's view on reference with respect to the dominant paradigm of reference that derives from the contrast between proper names and definite descriptions. Indexicals and demonstratives, instead of being a hybrid of them, provide an alternative approach to reference that naturally explains the meaning and use of our referential devices and, thus, the cognitive motivation and impact of utterances containing them. Indexicals and demonstratives are the topic of another chapter in this volume, and I don't want to be redundant. However, to give an accurate picture of Perry's view on names and descriptions, a brief discussion on roles, cognitive fixes and referential intentions is required, which naturally stems from an account of indexicals and demonstratives. I'll do that in §4. The longest section of the paper, §5, will be devoted to the referential expressions *par excellence*: proper names. I'll present Perry's concept of 'name-notion networks', the various contents of an utterance containing names that explain their cognitive motivation and impact, and his approach to vacuous names. §6 will be devoted to definite descriptions, whose *referential* use is naturally explained, I think, within Perry's approach. As we said above, §7 will discuss his concept of unarticulated constituents, when it comes to accounting for cases of reference without words. Finally, I'll draw some general conclusions in §8.

2 Semantics and Pragmatics of Reference

The name 'John Perry' designates John Perry, just as the definite description 'the author of "Reference and Reflexivity"' does.[1] I refer to John Perry when I utter the name 'John Perry', and I refer to John Perry as well when I utter the description 'the author of "Reference and Reflexivity"'. One can assume that it is in virtue of a two-place semantic relation between words and things that reference is possible: That seems to be the dominant view in much of the traditional philosophy of language, as influenced by formal semantics. The case of indexicals and demonstratives would just show that the referring relation is sometimes relative to a context of utterance, but reference would basically be a semantic relation between words and things.

The semantic view was challenged by Strawson (1950), who famously claimed that referring is not something that expressions (types) do, but that people do by using expressions. Kent Bach (2007) complains that Perry (2001B2) sometimes uses phrases like 'what an indexical refers to', suggesting the opposite. He rightly insists that we should not use phrases like 'what an indexical refers to', except as a shorthand of 'what a speaker refers to in using an indexical'. In his response to Bach, Perry makes explicit his agreement with Strawson:

> I believe it [Strawson's remark] is reflected in my theory in a number of ways: reference is a concept connected with content, which is a property of utterances, which are acts by people, not expression types. I do not say that indexicals such as 'I' refer, but that utterances of them do. ... One might say more generally, I suppose, that people accomplish things by acting, their acts don't accomplish anything. The National Rifle Association tells us that guns don't kill, people do; Bach can say, Charlton Heston-like, "acts don't refer to people, people do." But I can reply, "That's true, but people refer by performing intentional acts, that is, utterances, and utterances have properties that make it much easier to refer." If we want to cut down on murder, regulating guns is a good idea; if we want to cut

[1] From now on, 'to designate' should be taken as a neutral verb in contrast with 'to name', 'to denote', 'to describe', and 'to refer,' which are used to distinguish among different particular ways of designation. As we will see, Perry contributes to clarifying the differences.

> down on reference, eliminating utterances would go a long way. (Perry 2007c: 514)

Hence, there is no issue between Bach and Perry about whether referring is something words do (the semantic view) or something speakers do (the pragmatic view). They both adopt the second stance.

Still, there seems to be some difference in their view on reference; a difference that has to do with the role they attribute to the speaker's intention (and the hearer's uptake) in determining the referent. Bach says:

> ... there is no fact of the matter, independent of the speaker's referential intention, as to what a discretionary indexical refers to. There is no question as to what the reference is beyond what the speaker intends to refer to and what his audience takes him to refer to. (Bach 2007: 407)

According to Bach, then, with discretionary indexicals, the speaker refers to what he intends to refer to. And I think that Perry would again agree in this case, since Perry calls 'discretionary' precisely those indexicals whose referent is determined by the speaker's intention, contrasting them with 'automatic' indexicals whose referent is determined whatever the speaker's intention, by the meaning of the expression and objective facts of the context of utterance, except perhaps the intention to use the indexical with its conventional meaning (see Perry 2001B2: 58–63). Now, the only purely automatic indexical expression seems to be the first-person singular pronoun 'I'—the 'essential indexical'. And the only purely discretionary indexical expressions seem to be the demonstratives 'this', 'that', 'it', and (with some qualifications) 'he' and 'she'. Other expressions like 'you', 'here', 'now' and even 'today,' 'yesterday', or 'tomorrow' require both contextual facts and speaker's intention to fix their reference. And anyhow, except in the case of purely discretional demonstratives, in which, according to Perry[2] it is the speaker's *directing* intention that determines reference, there is more than the speaker's intentions involved in the determination of the reference of a referential expression: The conventional meaning of the expression used plays its role, and the circumstances of the utterance. That is, the context of utterance plays its role as well.

The latter derives from Perry's view of language as action, and from the corresponding central place acknowledged to utterances as the proper unit of study of semantics and pragmatics. As acts, utterances get their contents from three different sources: the plans (goals, beliefs, intentions) of the agent/speaker, the tools/words used, and the circumstances of the execution. One single movement by an agent can be taken to constitute various acts, relative to different aspects that are taken as given: In a single act we can

[2] Following Kaplan 1989b (not Kaplan 1989a).

distinguish a number of contents. I move my forefinger downwards; I press the letter 'J' on my computer keyboard; I produce the letter 'J' on the screen; I write the first letter of the name 'John'; I write the first letter of John Perry's name. By a single movement of my forefinger, I accomplished various things, given my intentions, the tools I used and various contextual facts. Not all those things would count as what I *did* in the relevant sense of doing at hand; but it is worth distinguishing them as relevant contents of my action, for an account of what I *did*.

Similarly, consider that I produce the sound '\jon\'; I utter the English name 'John'; I refer to John; I try to get John's attention. I accomplish various things by moving my mouth and tongue and other parts of my vocal articulatory system. Not all of them count as referring to John Perry, but they are worth distinguishing for an account of what I said, or whom I refer to and how.

In any event, we can say that all this results in a speaker-oriented theory of reference. Referring is something that speakers do; reference is determined as the joint product of the speaker's intentions, the conventional meaning of the words she uses, and the context of utterance; but the hearer's understanding plays no role. The hearer's uptake does not determine reference (as relevance theorists, for example, seem to suggest; Sperber and Wilson 1986/1995, Carston 2002); though, in a communicative setting, the speaker's intentions are intended to be recognized by the hearer. Reference is not determined jointly by speaker and hearer either (Clark 1996). Reference determination is not a collective action by speaker and hearer; but an individual action performed by the speaker, usually intended to be recognized by the hearer.

Perry's latest view on reference cannot be understood without considering his pluralistic approach to the contents of our utterances and thoughts, most forcefully presented in "Reference and Reflexivity" (2001B2) and further elaborated in "Critical Pragmatics" (Korta and Perry 2011B). In fact, the latter is basically motivated by Perry's elaboration on the proper account of reference, which, in a sense, involves a change of the traditional paradigms of reference.

3 The Paradigms of Reference

Proper names constituted for a long time the obvious paradigm of referential expressions. "The only names of objects which connote nothing are proper names; and these have, strictly speaking, no signification" famously claimed John Stuart Mill echoing medieval philosophy (Mill 1893: Ch. 1, §5). To begin with, proper names of people or places seem in many languages at first sight to be devoid entirely of anything we could call linguistic meaning—the meaning of proper names cannot be consulted in dictionaries. And if there are some that seem to have any—e.g. 'Portsmouth' or 'Dances with Wolves'—their meaning becomes irrelevant once we use them as proper names.[3] Without meaning, the only contribution of a proper name to the proposition expressed by an utterance containing it is its referent.

Proper names constitute the paradigm of referring for many philosophers, with the only semantic role of providing a reference. The natural contrast of the referential paradigm is provided by definite descriptions. A description like 'the brightest student of philosophy in the 2010-2011 academic year' has a meaning, compositionally determined by the meanings of its parts, and, if we follow Russell and many people after him, even if it might accurately describe a certain individual, the contribution of a definite description to the proposition expressed by an utterance of a sentence containing it is not an individual but an identifying condition; a property that uniquely identifies the individual. Or, in the now common terminology, descriptions do not refer, but denote.

Contrasting names with descriptions, we are comparing two aspects. On the one hand, we are considering the meaning relation between the expression and the individual that it designates. On the other hand, what is at stake is the contribution of the expression to the proposition expressed by an utterance of a sentence containing it; this amounts to the issue of whether the proposition expressed is a singular or object-dependent proposition instead of a general or object-independent proposition. Following Perry's terminology, referring vs. describing is a distinction about the kind of contribution terms make to the proposition expressed (an individual vs. an identifying condition); while naming vs. denoting is about the mechanism of designation (a conventional direct relation between the expression and the object *versus* an identifying condition provided by the meaning of the term). Names *name* and *refer*; descriptions *denote* and *describe*.[4]

These two paradigms can be summed up in the following table:[5]

[3] It is well-known that Russell went even further claiming that if an alleged proper name had any remnant of meaning, then it was not an actual proper name, but a disguised description. That left natural language without *logically* proper names except for 'this', 'that', and maybe 'I'.

[4] I am ignoring here referential uses of definite descriptions (Donnellan 1966). See §6 below.

[5] Perry (2001B2) acknowledges Martí (1995) for the insights here.

Table 3.1

	Refer	Describe
Name	Proper names	
Denote		Definite descriptions

Now, indexicals do not easily fit in this picture. They look like a hybrid of names and descriptions. An expression like 'I' seems to have a linguistic meaning that gives an identifying condition to select a unique individual, something like 'the speaker of this utterance'. So, in that respect 'I' is closer to a description than to a proper name, and the same goes for 'here' ('the place of this utterance'), 'now' ('the time of this utterance'), and so on. They can be said to denote and not name their designata. However, they seem to refer, not to describe: Utterances of sentences containing them express singular or object-dependent propositions. The table including indexicals would look like this:

Table 3.2

	Refer	Describe
Name	Proper names	
Denote	Indexicals	Definite descriptions

There is another way to look at these matters, though. Instead of starting from the paradigm provided by names and its contrast to descriptions, Perry puts forward an alternative paradigm on reference based on some features of indexicals and demonstratives that, even if essential to them, arguably, are also present in the use of names and descriptions.

The conventional meaning of indexicals exploits certain roles that objects (or places or times) play relative to the speaker producing an utterance: being the speaker of the utterance ('I'), being the time of the utterance ('now'), being the place of the utterance ('here'). These distinguished roles are especially useful for the speaker to refer to objects (or locations or moments) exploiting her *cognitive fixes*[6] on them. Using indexicals to refer basically consists in the following: using a term that exploits one's cognitive fix on an object ('the self', 'the present', 'the place I am at') in order for

[6] The term is taken from Wettstein 1991. Broadly speaking, a 'cognitive fix' on an object is a way of thinking of an object, from perception to thinking of it via a description to a name. One's cognitive fix on an object involves a role the object plays in one's life (see Korta and Perry 2011B: Ch. 3).

the hearer to get his own cognitive fix on that very object (e.g. 'the person in front of me', 'the present', 'the place we are at').

The case of demonstratives like 'this', 'that', or 'he' and 'she' is a bit different. Their conventional meaning gives us little more than 'the object/person I'm thinking about', but, in paradigmatic cases at least, the speaker exploits a perceptual cognitive fix she has on the object, intending that the hearer get his own cognitive fix.

Perry sticks to a referentialist view on indexicals and demonstratives. But he makes room for a plurality of contents of the utterance. In "Reference and Reflexivity" the main difference is between the *referential* content or truth-conditions and a variety of more or less reflexive or utterance-bound contents that he dubs 'indexical' (when indexicals and demonstratives are at stake), 'intentional' (for proper names), and 'designational' (for definite descriptions).

The 'official' or referential content of an utterance of a sentence containing a proper name, an indexical, or a demonstrative is a singular proposition with the object referred to as a constituent. That is why Perry is a referentialist. But, besides the referential content, we have a family of contents which, to use the terms of "Critical Pragmatics," involve linking the exploited and targeted cognitive fixes one has on the designated object (see Korta and Perry 2009 and 2011B: Ch. 3).

The use of indexicals and demonstratives as role-management devices seems clear and, if Perry is right, is also critical for explaining the use of proper names and descriptions. But before we address names and descriptions, it is worth saying a couple of words about the structure of referential intentions.

4 Roles and Referential Intentions

Perry's view on referential intentions is basically Gricean: They are hearer-oriented overt intentions intended to be recognized by the hearer. Using an expression *X* to designate an object *O* (the *primary* referential intention), the speaker exploits her own cognitive fix on *O*, involving a particular role *O* plays in her life, and intends the hearer to realize that. This is basically what Perry, echoing Kaplan 1989b, calls the *directing* intention. Now, the speaker's aim is that the hearer get his own cognitive fix on *O*. This is the *target* intention. The roles involved in the directing and the target intentions are somehow linked and the speaker intends the hearer to realize that. The *directing, target* and *path* intentions are the three main aspects that Korta and Perry distinguish in the structure of referential intentions (see Korta and

Perry 2011B: Ch. 4).[7] As we said earlier, indexicals are especially suited to exploit specific utterance-relative roles: the meaning of 'I', 'the speaker of this utterance', makes it especially suited to exploit the cognitive fix one has on oneself. The meaning of 'you' makes it particularly useful to designate the person the speaker is addressing. The meaning of 'that man' makes it especially useful to refer to a person that the speaker sees (perceptual cognitive fix).

Directing intentions are *determinative*, in the sense that the speaker will designate whatever or whomever plays the role she's exploiting. So, whatever her further intentions, they don't determine the referent:

> Basically, the speaker has authority over which role he exploits. But he does not have authority over who or what actually plays that role; if his beliefs about that are wrong, he may refer to a thing to which he does not intend to refer. (Korta and Perry 2011B: 42).

Moreover, the speaker not only attempts to refer to an object exploiting her cognitive fix on it, but typically also aims at some cognitive fix on the part of the hearer, via some more or less vague path. This *targeted* cognitive fix on the object by the hearer is critical for his inference of the (intended) implicatures of the utterance. The particular way of referring (with particular directive and target intentions) will affect the various implicatures carried by an utterance. This, of course, is critical to account for the cognitive motivation and impact of the use of referential terms (see Korta and Perry 2006).

Suppose I tell you in face-to-face conversation, "I leave on the 8:00 am plane." Using 'I', I'm exploiting a particular cognitive fix I have on me, 'self' (directing intention), and expect you to link the roles of 'speaker of the utterance' (path) with 'person I have in front of me' (target). That can be a good way to elicit a response like, "I can give you a ride to the airport." If, instead, I say, "Kepa leaves in the 8:00 am plane", I attempt a more complicated path involving a notion-network (see below), that can easily get an answer like, "So what? Doesn't he or she know the way to the airport?"

Since indexicality is the subject of another chapter, we should focus on other ways of referring. Their differences as role-managing devices, though, will be at the heart of Perry's account of their differences in cognitive motivation and impact.

---

[7] There we also distinguish the *grammatical* and the *auxiliary* intentions, which allow us to talk of the GDTPA structure of paradigm referential intentions. For the sake of simplicity, here I'm leaving these two out, but see footnote 8.

5 Proper Names

Contrary to what Russell claimed, it seems that in using a proper name to refer to an individual you don't need much information about the individual, once you know the expression is a proper name. Suppose I tell you now, "Larraitz is beautiful." Recognizing 'Larraitz' as a proper name allows you to ask "What is Larraitz?" or "Who is Larraitz?", and thus refer to the person or thing I refer to with my statement.[8] You can also google 'Larraitz' and find out that it is a name for a place, where there is a small church devoted to the Madonna with that name, and is traditionally also a name for women.[9]

You may individuate names by their bearers and consider that there are hundreds of homophonic but different names sounding 'Larraitz'. Or you can consider that there are hundreds of female humans, a place and a little church that share a single name. Perry's option is the latter. Proper names, according to him, are nambiguous (with an 'n'), which is a sort of ambiguity characteristic of names. Nambiguity is also resolved appealing to the speaker's intentions in using a name, but here, instead of a limited number of meanings, we can have hundreds, thousands or even millions of meanings. Central to Perry's account of the use of proper names in communication is the concept of a 'name-notion network'.

5.1 Names and Networks

For an individual to be referentially accessible to a speaker via a name 'N', the speaker needs to be able to utter "N" as a part of what Perry calls a 'name-notion network' (or 'network' for short). The idea is similar to Kripke's 'chains of communication', Donnellan's 'referential chains' or Chastain's 'anaphoric chains' (Kripke 1980, Donnellan 1970, Chastain 1975). Except in the few cases in which the speaker performs an act of 'baptism', in using a proper name the speaker intends to co-refer with a

---

[8] One can say that this shows that names are not just referential tags, as they present themselves as names. I think Perry would put it otherwise. It is a matter of the speaker's *grammatical intention* to use a word as a name, or a name as a subject (versus, say, a direct object) in a sentence. In other words, names do not present themselves, but speakers present them in uttering them. Nothing seems to prevent me from referring to a person with 'Swimming with dolphins' or by 'Microsoft'. Thanks to Eros Corazza for raising this issue. Incidentally, the latter was the name of one of the Perrys's cats. The other was called 'Macintosh'.

[9] In Basque, many personal names come from toponyms, and are genderless, except those where an appearance of the Holy Virgin was reported, like 'Larraitz', 'Arantzazu', 'Leire', 'Olatz', and so many others. For a view of proper names that takes them to include gender and other information, see Corazza 2011.

previous use of that name by another speaker, or at least intends to co-refer with a previous utterance of the name, if the previous utterance referred to anything. The practices of co-referring and conditional co-referring (or 'coco-referring' using Korta and Perry 2011B's term) form a network that supports a convention to refer to an individual with a name. A use of a name that exploits a convention refers to the origin of the network that supports the convention, if it has one; otherwise, the conventions and the use are empty.

If referring to an object using a name can just consist in an act of coco-referring, it seems to follow that there are very few conditions on referring via names, and this seems right. In particular, you don't need an utterance-independent description that identifies the referent, as we said above.

But names can also point to information that one has about an individual. Names also involve cognitive fixes we have on objects. A nominal cognitive fix involves a name, a (detached) notion associated with the name that involves all sorts of information (and possibly misinformation) about the object, and a network of which that notion is a part. The object plays a role in the life of a person, in virtue of having such a cognitive fix.

5.2 Names, Roles and Contents

Names are not as clearly related to perceptual and utterance-relative roles as demonstratives and indexicals are. But they also work as role-management devices. Suppose the famous actress Julia Roberts sits to my right at dinner, and tells me she wants the salt.[10] The salt-shaker is by my left but out of my reach so I tell John,

(1) Julia Roberts would like the salt.

John, like practically all movie-lovers in the world, has a nominal cognitive fix with the name 'Julia Roberts', a detached notion of her, and an accessible network. In this case, I expect John to link that notion with a buffer or a perceptual cognitive fix of her as 'the person sitting to Kepa's right', so that he hands me the salt-shaker and I satisfy Julia's desire for salt. Here I exploit my nominal cognitive fix on Julia Roberts and aim at John's role-linking between his own nominal cognitive fix on her (path) and his perceptual cognitive fix on her as the person to my right (target).

Suppose now that after the conference reception, John is tired and asks me if someone could drive him to the hotel. I say,

(2) Larraitz is very nice.

[10] This is a variation on an example by Korta and Perry 2009, 2011B.

Let's suppose he recognizes 'Larraitz' as a proper name for a person but knows nothing about its bearer. On the basis only of his knowledge of English, he would only understand what Perry calls the 'reflexive' or 'utterance-bound' truth-conditions of my utterance:

Utterance-bound truth-conditions

> Given that (2) is in English, has the syntax it does, and 'is very nice' means what it does in English, (2) is true if and only if
>
> ∃*x*, ∃*N*, ∃*y* such that *x* is the speaker of (2), *N* is the network *x* exploits with 'Larraitz', *y* is the origin of *N* and *y* is very nice.

Of course, he heard me saying it, and recognized me, Kepa, as the speaker of (2), so he understood something like:

Speaker-bound truth-conditions

> Given that (2) is in English, has the syntax it does, 'is very nice' means what it does in English, and Kepa is the speaker of (2), (2) is true if and only if
>
> ∃*N*, ∃*y* such that *N* is the network Kepa exploits with 'Larraitz', *y* is the origin of *N* and *y* is very nice.

Now, suppose that John remembers nothing about $\mathbf{N}_{\text{Larraitz}}$, except that it's the network I'm exploiting by my use of 'Larraitz'. In that case, we could describe the content he gets from (2) as:

Network-bound truth-conditions

> Given that (2) is in English, has the syntax it does, 'is very nice' means what it does in English, Kepa is the speaker of (2), and $\mathbf{N}_{\text{Larraitz}}$ is the network Kepa exploits with 'Larraitz', (2) is true if and only if
>
> ∃*y* such that *y* is the origin of $\mathbf{N}_{\text{Larraitz}}$ and *y* is very nice.

Knowing the network-bound truth-conditions doesn't count as understanding what I said by (2), but John will still be in position to refer to Larraitz, that is, to coco-refer with my utterance, for instance, by asking, "Who is Larraitz?" The network-bound truth-conditions are probably what we most often understand when understanding an utterance containing a proper name. And that is probably all we rely on to produce an utterance containing a proper name. Contrary to what Russell claimed, we need not be acquainted with the bearer of the name to use and understand the use of proper names. Now, for various reasons, we keep the concept of what is said (the proposition expressed, the content) to apply to the content that includes the referent itself; to what Perry calls the referential truth-conditions of the utterance.

If John remembers something about Larraitz, namely, the origin of the network $\mathbf{N}_{\text{Larraitz}}$, he will get what I said, the official content of (2) or its

Referential truth-conditions

> Given that (2) is in English, has the syntax it does, 'is very nice' means what it does in English, Kepa is the speaker of (2), $\mathbf{N}_{\text{Larraitz}}$ is the network Kepa exploits with 'Larraitz' and *y* is the origin of $\mathbf{N}_{\text{Larraitz}}$, (2) is true if and only if
>
> *y* is very nice.

To sum up, Perry's view on proper names is a referentialist view, in the sense that he considers the 'official' content of an utterance containing a proper name to be a singular proposition, a proposition constituted by the individual named, and not by any description associated to it.

Now, even though names do not involve any description uniquely selecting the individual referred to, naming involves a network of utterances and (possibly thin) notions that supports coco-referring. If the network has an origin, we manage to refer to an individual. If it doesn't, we don't refer (and, then, we don't co-refer) to anything. But the plurality of contents and the use of names as role-management devices explain our use of names in both cases, that is, the cognitive significance of co-referring names, and the content of empty names. We turn to this now.

5.3 Names and Roles

Suppose that John's take on (2) didn't go further than the network-bound truth-conditions of my utterance, and he asked, "Who is Larraitz?", thus coco-referring (and co-referring) to Larraitz. My answer could be something like

> (3) She is Larraitz.

gesturing towards Larraitz. The traditional referentialist account of demonstratives and proper names has problems in accounting for the cognitive impact and the cognitive effect of identity statements like this. If both the demonstrative and the name refer to an individual, and that's all they contribute to the proposition expressed, then (3) would just express the identity of an individual to herself. But, why should anyone utter an utterance expressing a self-identity? How could anyone get information from an utterance expressing that an individual is identical to herself?

This is how Perry explains it. The referential truth-conditions of (3) involve just the self-identity of Larraitz. I could have expressed the same proposition uttering "Larraitz is Larraitz" or "She is she". Uttering (3), though, I help John link two different roles, or two distinct cognitive fixes, on Larraitz: one perceptual, the other nominal. The former is linked by my utterance of 'she' at the level of speaker-bound truth-conditions: from 'the person Kepa has in mind', through 'the person Kepa is gesturing towards', to 'the woman I see in that corner'. The second is linked via John's nominal notion on Larraitz, which might include some information like, 'Basque linguist, former student of Kepa's' but not enough to identify her in the room. (3) allows him now to identify Larraitz. This explains the informativeness of (3), without giving up the referentialist picture on names and demonstratives.

5.4 Empty Names

Perry's family of utterance-contents gives a natural account of utterances containing vacuous or empty names. These would constitute name-notion networks with no origin; that is, going up in the network from a present use to its origin, we end up in a 'block' (using Donnellan 1974's terminology): we end up finding no origin. This means that utterances containing empty names lack referential truth-conditions. But, of course, in Perry's account this doesn't mean they lack any kind of content at all.

If I sincerely utter something like

(4) Atlantis was a wonderful city.

you would be right in saying that my utterance has no referential truth-conditions, since there is nothing that counts as the origin of the Atlantis network. Still, you could be right in claiming that my utterance is false. You would be judging the network-bound truth-conditions of (4), something like:

> Given that (4) is in English, has the syntax it does, 'was a wonderful city' means what it does in English, Kepa is the speaker of (4), and $\mathbf{N}_{\text{Atlantis}}$ is the network Kepa exploits with 'Atlantis', (4) is true if and only if
>
> $\exists y$ such that y is the origin of $\mathbf{N}_{\text{Atlantis}}$ and y was a wonderful city.

Now, obviously, the inexistence of such an origin makes (4) false, and makes the statement of such inexistence true:

(5) Atlantis didn't exist.

Again, we cannot explain the (contingent) truth of (5) by its referential truth-conditions (it has none). Our intuitions would be accounted for by appealing to its network-bound truth-conditions:

$\neg\exists y$ such that y is the origin of $\mathbf{N}_{\text{Atlantis}}$.

Perry's account of fiction and fictional names in non-existential contexts takes a different route. He takes that an utterance like

(6) Watson asked Holmes to quit the use of cocaine.

should not be judged true or false, but accurate or inaccurate relative to the corpus of Doyle's stories about Holmes. But space limits oblige us to leave these issues for Dr. Watson—or for Perry himself.[11]

6 Definite Descriptions

Donnellan 1966's distinction between attributive and referential uses is one of the most recurrent in discussions about definite descriptions. Perry's view is quite close to Donnellan's in how it locates the critical difference between the two kinds of use at the level of the speaker's intentions. But it is finer-grained when spelling out the difference. In short, the speaker's directing, path, and target intentions in the attributive use involve a mere descriptive fix on the individual. On the referential use, even if the path intention involves the descriptive fix, the directing and target intentions are about a perceptual or notional fix the speaker exploits and expects the hearer to have.

The distinction can be made clearer using the various kinds of utterance contents. So far we had utterance-bound, speaker-bound, network-bound and referential truth-conditions of an utterance. Referential truth-conditions is the level that usually corresponds to the proposition expressed or the content of the utterance (when mono-propositionalism is assumed). At this level, Perry follows a Russellian (though not exactly Russell's) theory of descriptions, in that they include an identifying condition of the individual, not the individual itself. According to Korta and Perry (2011B: 94), the *referential truth-conditions* of an utterance **u** of 'Smith's murderer is insane' would be the following ones:

[11] Perry briefly discusses the case of fictional names like 'Sherlock Holmes' in 2001B2: Ch. 8, 170–2.

> Given that **u** is in English, its syntax, the meaning of the words, and the fact that Smith is the origin of the exploited Smith-network, **u** is true if and only if there is a unique person who murdered Smith, and that person is insane.

This would be the content of the utterance when the speaker is looking at Smith's mutilated body, and with nobody in mind, she utters **u**. The content of the belief she wants to impart is that whoever murdered Smith is insane. Her target cognitive fix is just descriptive.

Now, in the referential case, speaker and hearer are at the trial of Jones, who, let's assume, did actually murder Smith. Watching Jones's strange behavior, the speaker intends to impart the belief that Jones is insane by her utterance **u'** of 'Smith's murderer is insane'. In this case, the speaker aims at the *designational* or *referential* truth-conditions* of her utterance:

> Given that **u'** is in English, its syntax, the meaning of the words, the fact that Smith is the origin of the exploited Smith-network, and the fact that Jones murdered Smith, **u'** is true if and only if Jones is insane.

This amounts to a singular proposition with Jones as a constituent. Now, the difference between a referential and an attributive use of 'Smith's murderer' is in the speaker's intention, as Donnellan suggested. Is the speaker intending to impart the referential* truth-conditions of her utterance? Or is she just intending the hearer's understanding to stop at the referential truth-conditions? Or both?

The last is a real option. Whenever there is an individual uniquely satisfying a description, an utterance containing it will have both referential and referential* contents. The latter has to be true for the former to be true. And that can be the speaker's intention: using a description essentially to designate the individual that uniquely fits the description. So, Perry's account allows a double attributive-referential use of a description. When there is no intention to use the description essentially, but just as a means—as good as a name, a demonstrative, or a complex demonstrative—to designate Jones, we would have a referential use, in which the speaker intentionally imparts the referential* truth-conditions of her utterance. When the speaker just wants to impart a descriptive cognitive fix with no further target intention, her use is merely attributive.

The description 'Smith's murderer' is a complete description, since it provides an identifying condition that applies to one and only one individual. But most often we use incomplete definite descriptions like 'the table', 'my neighbor', 'the book', 'the computer', which are insufficient to pick out a unique individual. Perry's account of incomplete descriptions goes along with his concept of unarticulated constituents. We turn now to discuss them.

7 Unarticulated Constituents

One of Perry's best-known contributions to the toolbox of basic concepts in the philosophy of language and mind is the concept of 'unarticulated constituents', a concept that has been described, somewhat derogatorily, as a 'myth' by Cappelen and Lepore 2007.[12] As Perry says, his original insight in his paper "Thought without Representation" (1986d) was not directly related to the content of utterances, but to the content of a particular kind of thoughts, 'self-less' thoughts, whose truth-conditions seemed to clearly involve the thinker even if they didn't require the self to be represented. Thus a thought expressible by "He's to the right" and a thought expressible by "He's to *my* right" would share their truth-conditional content, involving the thinker, but in different ways: via a representation (articulated) in the latter; without a representation (unarticulated) in the former. Perry thought that self-less thoughts were important for theories of perception and action and that they were likely to be the only kind of thoughts of non-human animals, small human children, and even adult humans in many circumstances.

As an illustration, he gives the example of a telephone conversation with his son Joe on their plans to play tennis in Palo Alto. Joe tells John, "It's raining", thereby conveying that they should postpone their plans. Perry remarks:

> What my son said was true, because it was raining in Palo Alto. ... In order to assign a truth-value to my son's statement, as I just did, I needed a place. ... So Palo Alto is a constituent of the content of my son's remark, which no component of his statement designated: it is an *unarticulated* constituent. (Perry 1986d/2000: 172)

A vast literature on meteorological reports was thus initiated. And beyond meteorological reports, the analysis of other cases of elements of what is said that get pragmatically determined, or are so considered by many, like grading adjectives, quantifier domain restrictions, incomplete definite descriptions, subsentential utterances, and a long *et cetera*.[13] Unarticulated constituents have been essentially accepted and considered a case of implicitures (Bach) or part of the explicature via pragmatic enrichment (relevance theory), or neglected to be really articulated in the sentence's logical

[12] Perry (2007c: 539), quotes from a previous version of Cappelen and Lepore's paper, in which they call the unarticulated constituent position "to say the least, trendy... all the rage in philosophical and linguistic circles". But the phrase was withdrawn from the last and published version. Perry says he loved the paragraph in question too much to give it up (573, Fn. 17).

[13] This literature includes work by Bach (2004, 2006), Barwise (1988), Borg (2005), Corazza and Dokic (2010), Crimmins and Perry (1989b), Neale (2007), Recanati (2002, 2004, 2007a), Stanley (2000, 2002), Taylor (2001, 2007), and many more.

form (indexicalism), or just considered external to semantic content along with implicatures (minimalists or Cappelen and Lepore).

After all these years, I think that Perry would qualify some of the views that are attributed to him and have some prevalence in the discussion about the topic, at least concerning the case of examples like 'It's raining'. These are cases of utterances of grammatically complete sentences that express a proposition allegedly including an element (a place) that is not designated by any sentential component. The first qualification concerns the claim that without the provision of the unarticulated constituent, the place of the raining event, the utterance lacks truth-conditional content. The quote above says that. And he has often repeated the same idea:

> In this case, I say that the place is an *unarticulated constituent* of the proposition expressed by the utterance. It is a constituent, because, since rains occur at a time in a place, there is no truth-evaluable proposition unless a place is supplied. It is unarticulated, because there is no morpheme that designates that place (Perry 2001B2: 45)

This idea has been a salient theme in the debate about unarticulated constituents. Cappelen and Lepore 2005 insist that this is wrong. They claim that an utterance of 'It is raining' expresses the proposition that it is raining, which is true if and only if it is raining. Period. They admit that that is not what the speaker usually means in uttering it. This would usually include the place of the event, but it would not constitute the *semantic* content (the proposition *semantically* expressed) by an utterance of 'It is raining', which would be truth-conditionally complete.

Most people disagree. Recanati argues that a process of saturation (or enrichment) is needed to get a truth-conditionally complete proposition. Bach calls the proposition semantically expressed by 'It is raining' a *propositional radical*, insisting on its propositional incompleteness. Stanley agrees but poses a *hidden* indexical that would articulate the location of the event. But I think that nowadays Perry would somehow acknowledge that, involuntarily, he might have caused some sterile discussion on semantic *incompleteness*. Following his most recent work on the semantics and pragmatics of reference, he could reformulate his previous claims in the following way:

Joe's utterance of

(7) It is raining,

without the provision of the raining location, lacks *referential* truth-conditions. But that does not mean that it is truth-conditionally incomplete, because it would have utterance-bound *complete* truth-conditions:

> Given that (7) is in English, that it has the syntax it does, and that 'It is raining' means what it does in English, (7) is true if and only if
>
> $\exists x$, $\exists y$ such that x is the speaker of (7), y is the place x has in mind, and it is raining at y.[14]

This is not what Joe stated in uttering (7). What he said would be given by its referential truth-conditions:

> Given that (7) is in English, that it has the syntax it does, that 'It is raining' means what it does in English, and that Joe has Palo Alto in mind, (7) is true if and only if
>
> It is raining at Palo Alto.

Both the utterance-bound and the referential truth-conditions (as well as the speaker-bound truth-conditions, given by the fact that Joe is the speaker of (7)) do have an unarticulated constituent—an existentially closed location parameter in the former, a place in the latter—because, *pace* Stanley, it is not articulated in the sentence uttered. But providing the particular place is not required for the utterance to have a truth-conditionally complete content. This only prevents it from having a *referential* content.

What about the semantic content of (7)? I think Perry's answer would be quite straightforward now. Sentences do not have content; sentences do not have truth-conditions. Utterances do. A variety of contents, given by the conventional meaning of the sentence uttered plus various facts about the context of utterance, starting with the fact that an utterance of that sentence has been made. This provides the utterance-bound content of the utterance, which is a natural candidate for the category of *semantic content*, at least from a minimalist approach to semantics that seeks to keep the pragmatic 'intrusion' into semantics to a minimum. On the other hand, the speaker's intentions are critical to determine the *referential* truth-conditions of the utterance, which shouldn't come as a surprise, if we depart *ab initio* from a pragmatic view on reference that assumes that words do not refer, but rather that people use them to refer.

---

14 One can argue that so formulated, we are *articulating* the location at the level of the speaker's mind. Two qualifications are in order here. First, I am limiting the discussion to the issue of (un)articulation in utterances, and nothing prevents the contents of (7) from having unarticulated constituents that are articulated at the level of the speaker's thought. Second, 'to have in mind' should be understood in a broad sense. Suppose I'm thinking 'He's to the right'. The truth-conditions would include me, and, in that sense, I would have myself in mind, without necessarily having myself articulated in my thought. See more about Perry's recent view on unarticulated constituents in language and thought in Korta and Perry 2011B, Ch. 9. Thanks again to Eros Corazza for raising this issue.

There is much more to say about the various concepts of unarticulated constituents and their multifarious applications, but it will have to wait for another occasion.

8 Conclusions

From “Frege on Demonstratives” (1977) onward, Perry’s work on reference has been profound and influential. He focuses on the meaning and use of demonstratives and indexicals, with particular attention to the first-person pronoun ‘I’, which is central to his reflection on personal identity. It is not surprising then that his view on indexicals as role-managing devices ended up constituting the main paradigm of reference that provides a natural framework for understanding the use of proper names and descriptions. His study on essential indexicals and ‘I-thoughts’ led him to the concept of unarticulated constituents. I have tried to give a fair account of his current views. But I feel that doing justice to his work, methods and findings exceeds my limited capacities. In “The Adventure of the Abbey Grange,” Holmes tells his friend:

> I must admit you have some power of selection, which atones for much which I deplore in your narratives. Your fatal habit of looking at everything from the point of view of a story instead of as a scientific exercise has ruined what might have been an instructive and even classical series of demonstrations. You slur over work of the utmost finesse and delicacy, in order to dwell upon sensational details which may excite, but cannot possibly instruct, the reader.

Perry never told me anything like that. And I guess he never will. But he might have thought it. Or he might after reading this. Fortunately, in this case, the readers can and ought to go through Perry’s writings themselves, as a corrective to my humble and clumsy mediation.

Acknowledgements

I am particularly indebted to John Perry for his constant support and inspiration. I am also grateful to my colleagues of the group ‘Language as Action: Semantics, Pragmatics, and Rhetoric’ at the Institute for Logic, Cognition, Language and Information (ILCLI) for their comments and criticisms, especially to Eros Corazza, Joana Garmendia, María Ponte and Larraitz Zubeldia. Thanks also to Jérôme Dokic and Neil Van Leeuwen for their comments and suggestions. This work was partially supported by a grant of the Basque Government (IT323-10) and the Spanish Ministry of Science and Innovation (FFI2009-08574).

4

Perry on Propositional Attitude Reports

ALBERT NEWEN

1 The Phenomenon

On the basis of a person's utterance or explicit acceptance of an utterance or explicit acceptance of an utterance we often ascribe beliefs, desires, hopes, or other propositional attitudes. A propositional attitude report, e.g., "Frege believes that Venus is a planet", has the paradigmatic structure that a subject, here: Frege, has an attitude, here: a belief, with a propositional content, here: that Venus is a planet. It is a question of debate what exactly is the best syntactic and semantic analysis of attitude ascription: There are basically distinguished two lines of analysis. According to a relational analysis a belief report distinguishes the subject, the belief relation and some entities that characterize the content. According to an adverbial analysis, a belief report starts with a sentence operator "Frege believes that" and has as complement a sentence characterizing the content (Recanati 2000). In line with Perry we adopt the analysis of propositional attitude reports as relational and we introduce his view by focusing, as usual, on propositional attitude reports (as a paradigmatic case for all propositional attitude reports).

One basic background principle is the *principle of disquotation*: If a normal English speaker, on reflection, sincerely assents to 'p', then he believes that p.[1] If Betty utters "Herbert Frahm is born in Lübeck", we are

[1] In the case of indexicals there are transformations necessary, e.g., if Peter utters "I am hungry", then we are justified to make the report: "Peter believes that he himself is hungry". A

Identity, Language, and Mind: An Introduction to the Philosophy of John Perry.
Albert Newen and Raphael van Riel (eds.).

justified to make the following ascription: "Betty believes that Herbert Frahm is born in Lübeck". Betty made this utterance because she was a former neighbour of young Herbert Frahm, but she did not notice that he changed his name during the Nazi regime and called himself since then "Willy Brandt". Willy Brandt became a famous German chancellor and Betty noticed him in the news without registering that Herbert Frahm is identical with Willy Brandt. Given her information, Betty accepts both sentences "Willy Brandt is a German chancellor" and "Herbert Frahm is not a German chancellor" (she thinks that he is just a normal citizen of Lübeck she lost contact with after early childhood). Given her acceptance and denials, we receive the following true sentences:

(1) Betty believes that Willy Brandt is a German chancellor.
(2) Betty believes that Herbert Frahm is not a German chancellor.
(3) Herbert Frahm is identical with Willy Brandt.

The ignorance of identities produces a problem if we furthermore accept the following background principles:

(i) *Theory of direct reference:* The contribution of a proper name *n* to the semantic content of the belief expressed by a sentence containing *n* is the object referred to by the use of *n*.

According to this background principle, co-referring names like "Herbert Frahm" and "Willy Brandt" make the same semantic contribution to the content of the respective beliefs expressed. But then it seems that we ascribe Betty the belief that p and the belief that not-p at the same time. This, however, is unacceptable since (almost)[2] everyone accepts a *principle of minimal rationality*, which entails that no person can simultaneously have a (conscious) belief that p and a contradictory (conscious) belief that not-p. Why should we not simply give up the theory of direct reference for proper names (and indexicals)?

There are powerful arguments developed by Saul Kripke (1980). We will briefly consider the modal argument for proper names in simple (non-attitude-reporting sentences). It rejects the view that the meaning of the proper name "Aristotle" in a normal sentence, like "Aristotle is identical with K", can be expressed by a contingent description K that is true of Aris-

---

more generalized version of the principle of disquotation might take the following form: If a person sincerely, reflectively and competently utters or accepts a sentence *s* (under circumstances properly related to a context c), then A believes at time t in the context c what *s* expresses in c.

[2] In logic there is one development that tries to allow for some inconsistencies without losing all constraints; this is the paraconsistent logic. This way out is ignored in this overview.

totle. The argument against the view that a contingent description K runs as follows, where I use the description "the famous scholar of Plato" as a candidate for K:

(K1) It is necessary that Aristotle is identical with Aristotle.
(K2) It is not necessary that Aristotle is identical with the famous scholar of Plato.
(K3) But the meaning of the word "Aristotle" can be substituted salva veritate in any modal context (i.e. an utterance that starts with "It is necessary true that..."). Thus, we should be able to substitute the description "the famous scholar of Plato" with the name if the former would express the meaning of the latter.[3]
(K4) Therefore: The contingent description "the famous scholar of Plato" does not express the meaning of the name "Aristotle".

Kripke argues that the only alternative to the rejected account is the view that the meaning of a proper name is only the object referred to.

2 The Fregean Strategy

One way to argue that K1-K3 are true without ascribing contradictory beliefs to Betty is to argue that a name in a belief report makes a different semantic contribution than in other contexts. This was actually Frege's strategy: He takes belief ascriptions to be special contexts in which the semantic contribution of a name is no longer the object referred to but a mode of presentation of the object, i.e. a way of grasping an object typically expressed by a description. Betty thinks of Herbert Frahm as *the boy who lived in the same street in Lübeck when she was six years old.* So the description in italics expresses the mode of presentation such that the belief ascribed by (2) has roughly the content that the boy who lived in the same street in Lübeck when she was six years old is not a German chancellor. In the case of ascription (1), a different mode of presentation is relevant, i.e. *the leading social democrat who won the election in Germany in 1969.* Thus according to (1) Betty also believes that the leading social democrat who won the election in 1969 is a German chancellor. But these are not contradictory beliefs because we are dealing not with the situation of ascribing p and ascribing not p. We can describe this in a different way: The fact that Betty is unaware of the co-reference of the two definite descriptions (in

[3] That this is a correct principle can be illustrated by analyzing the word "grandfather". It means "being a father of a father or a father of a mother." The latter is giving us the meaning of "grandfather" because the following is true: "It is necessary that *being a grandfather* is identical with *being a father of a father or a father of a mother.*"

our actual world) is compatible with our intuitive evaluation that she is still minimally rational. The Fregean strategy consists basically in a shift of reference in the special case of attitude reports such that the semantic contribution of a proper name to the belief expressed is no longer the object referred to but a different entity, i.e. a mode of presentation of the object.

One central problem of the Fregean strategy is that when Betty utters "Herbert Frahm is not a German chancellor" she attributes a property to the person Herbert Frahm and not to a mode of presentation of Herbert Frahm, and there is a strong intuition that this does not change in the case of the report. This intuition becomes even more pressing in the case of indexicals. If I make the attribution "Betty believes that *I* am a nice person", I need not have any hint which mode of presentation Betty has of me. The sentence indicates no mode of presentation at all; there simply may be none, or we can imagine that we may still be confronted with a great variety of modes of presentations Betty has of me. Which one would be the relevant one? These considerations lead to problems of a multiplicity of modes of presentation or a complete lack of modes of presentation. And we have the strong intuition that with a proper name we express a belief about a person and this does not change in the case of belief reports.

According to these intuitions, we should at least accept for proper names and indexicals the theory of direct reference and a principle of semantic innocence which excludes a semantic shift in the case of attitude reports including names:

(ii) *Principle of semantic innocence:* The semantic contribution of a name or an indexical n that is part of a sentence s uttered in context c *is the same for all utterances* of sentences s containing n.

If we combine the latter with the principle of direct reference we obtain the following.

(iii) *Semantic innocence and direct reference:* The semantic contribution of a name or an indexical n that is part of a sentence s uttered in context c is the object referred to by n in c for all utterances of sentences s containing n.

3 Perry's Early Solution: A Naïve Russellian Strategy

Russell famously defended the view that sentences like "Willy Brandt was a German chancellor" and "Herbert Frahm was a German chancellor" express the same belief that can be characterized by the structured content <the person Willy Brandt; the property of being a German chancellor>. This means that these utterances have the same truth-condition, namely that the person Willy Brandt (which is actually identical with the person Herbert Frahm) is a German chancellor. But presupposing semantic innocence, it follows that according to the ascriptions (1) and (2), Betty believes p and the contradiction not-p at the same time. To maintain that Betty is minimally rational the naïve Russellians have to offer a way out.

One solution is essentially inspired by the early work of John Perry discussing the problems of indexicality (Perry 1977 and 1979a). Perry argues that to account for the difference between

(4) "I am hungry" uttered by Ernst Mach, and
(5) "Ernst Mach is hungry",

we have to distinguish between the *belief content* and the *belief state*. The belief content is a structured proposition that for a proper name or an indexical n contains as one component the object referred to by the use of n. The belief state is a cognitive particular that allows us to characterize the behavioral disposition of an individual. Let us have a look at the example: (4) and (5) have the same belief content, i.e. <the person Ernst Mach; the property of being hungry>. But the belief state expressed by both utterances is different. If Ernst Mach is suffering from a severe amnesia and has forgotten his name, he may believe that Ernst Mach is hungry without thereby having the disposition to go to the fridge to find some food. But if Mach believes that he himself is hungry he has exactly this disposition (given the standard background beliefs and -desires). The belief state involves some way of having a belief content. So, to account for the disposition of a person expressed by a belief report, we have to consider the *belief state* which consists in the belief content and a way of having it. Given these considerations, we may revise the principle of minimal rationality because the important aspect is that we should not accept that someone has contradictory dispositions at the same time although he may accept contradictory belief contents, e.g. because the latter are coarse grained and allow for different ways of having them. Since we can have the same belief content in different ways, we should introduce a *specific principle of minimal rationality*: A person is irrational if she believes a content p and its negation at the same time *in the same way*.

This revised criterion is not violated if we have a look at the attitude reports (1) and (2) since the same belief content <the person Willy Brandt; the property of being a German chancellor> is held in different ways, i.e. the utterances express two different *belief states* involving the same *belief content*.

How does the naïve Russellian account evaluate the truth and falsity of the relevant reports (1) and (2)? This is important because this is immediately connected with the question of how this theory deals with the substitution of co-referential names or indexicals in belief reports. A special version focusing on the *substitution of names and indexicals* claims the following: Since the semantic contribution of a name or an indexical is only the object referred to, two sentences in which we only substitute co-referential names or indexicals have via compositionality the same semantic content and therefore the same truth-value. More concisely: *A co-referential name or indexical can always be substituted in a sentence without change of the truth-value of the sentence (substitution salva veritate).* According to this principle the truth-value of (1) and (1a) has to be the same:

(1) Betty believes that Willy Brandt is a German chancellor.
(1a) Betty believes that Herbert Frahm is a German chancellor.

But according to our intuitions about Betty's belief system (1) is true while (1a) is false. Naïve Russellians claim that both reports are true and take this to be the real semantically determined truth-value of these reports. To account for the common intuition that (1a) is false while (1) is true, they have to consider pragmatic priniciples (transfers from what is said, the literal meaning of a utterance, e.g. "Peter has a nice handwriting", to what is actually meant by the utterance, e.g. "Peter is not able to do the job he applied for"; Grice 1975 and 1989). Such principles explain our widespread intuitions concerning the truth-values of (1) and (1a) on the level of pragmatically enriched contents. To put it in other words: Naïve Russellians claim that the semantic content of what is said by (1) and (1a) is the same and the difference is due to what is meant by the speaker. This strategy has received several criticisms. To highlight one let us have a look at beliefs concerning Fregean identity statements:

(6) Lois believes that Superman is stronger than Clark Kent.
(6a) Lois believes that Superman is stronger than Superman.

Since the step from (6) to (6a) is only an exchange of the co-referential names "Clark Kent" and "Superman", the naive Russellian has to evaluate both sentences as having the same truth-value. If (6) is true (6a) must also be true. But our strong intuition is that (6) is true while (6a) is false. And it is very implausible to claim that our evaluation that (6a) is false is based on a pragmatic implicature. It is much simpler to accept that the falsity of (6a) is part of the semantics of understanding the words and their composition, since we never believe that a person is stronger than herself. There is a strong intuition that this evaluation needs only a consideration of the literal sentence meaning, and does not rest on pragmatic principles.

Perry was never really committed to this naïve Russellian approach to truth-value evaluation, but his early view was close to it, since a detailed characterization of *belief states* was lacking. But Perry's important distinction between *belief content* and *belief state* already contained the potential to be developed into an independent sophisticated theory of attitude reports.

4 Perry's Sophisticated Neo-Russellianism: Introducing Unarticulated Constituents

The most important additional moves of Perry in his paper co-authored with Crimmins (Crimmins/Perry 1989) are the following: First, they distinguished two kinds of contents of a belief. (1) the *Russellian proposition expressed by an utterance*, and (2) the *Russellian proposition together with unarticulated constituents*, where the latter specifies a way of presenting the former. The unarticulated constituent enable them to characterize the belief state by introducing a special content. Secondly, Perry argues that in the case of belief reports the semantic content of the utterance is not the Russellian proposition expressed alone but it also contains relevant unarticulate constituents. Thirdly, the unarticulate constituents in the case of belief reports are mental entities, and they have to be characterized in the framework of beliefs, notions, and ideas. Let us spell this view out.

The first move keeps the account in the Neo-Russellian camp. Perry still accepts the Russellian view that the sentences

(7) "Willy Brandt is a German chancellor", and
(8) "Herbert Frahm is a German chancellor",

express the same Russellian proposition, i.e. <the person Willy Brandt; the property of being a German chancellor>. The names contribute only the object referred to as part of the proposition expressed and this will remain true for attitude reports as well. Thus, Perry and Crimmins accept the theory of direct reference for proper names in all contexts. But they do not accept the principle of substitution *salva veritate* for proper names in general. Although the substitution of the co-referential names in the two extensional sentences above, (7) and (8), does not change the truth-condition, this is the case when we consider (1) and (1a). So, the substitution principle is no longer valid for all contexts. Perry and Crimmins clearly leave the naïve Russellian position behind when accepting that the belief ascription (1) is true while (1a) is false. But what is the reason for the change of content that allows for the sentences having different truth-values?

Since Perry and Crimmins keep the theory of direct reference for names and indexicals, the semantic contribution of the co-referential names is still in part the same in the attitude reports, i.e. the object referred to by the names. But what is it that produces the difference in semantic content, given that the other words in the reports (1) and (1a) besides the names are all the same? The answer is that they take the believe-predicate syntactically to be a two-place predicate but it expresses a three place relation between a subject, a Russellian proposition, and an unarticulated constituent, which characterizes a way of grasping the relevant proposition.

The idea of unarticulated constituents is taken from observations about indexicals. An utterance of the sentence

(9) "It is raining",

is always understood in relation to relevant contextual features of place and time. Thus the utterance is usually taken to be equivalent to "It is raining here and now". The utterance (9) has unarticulated constituents of place and time, which are filled in by the contextual background (and sometimes additional constraints).[4] Perry and Crimmins claim that belief reports have a semantic content that contains an unarticulated constituent that is indicated by the belief predicate, which expresses a three place relation. The relevant unarticulated constituent is a mental entity (or a number of mental entities) that determines a way of having a Russellian proposition.

To complete the picture we need a short outline of the metaphysics of beliefs and their constituents. According to Crimmins and Perry, beliefs are concrete cognitive particulars that are constituted by notions and ideas. As concrete particulars these entities always belong to one person, just as a headache as a mental particular is always a headache of someone. They distinguish two components of a standard belief expressed by a sentence like "Willy Brandt is a German chancellor": notions and ideas. A notion is a cognitive component that is expressed by a singular term *referring to an object*, while an idea is a cognitive component that is expressed by a predicate *referring to a property.* The idea has the object referred to as its content, and the notion has the property referred to as its content. In the case of Betty she thinks of Willy Brandt as the representative of Germany who symbolically went down on his knees in Warsaw to start real peace between

---

[4] Sometimes additional shared knowledge of speaker and listener can be relevant, too. Suppose, I am uttering "It is raining" when I am in Bochum, phoning John Perry at Stanford. It can be the case that this utterance is made by me to inform John who is working in a cellar without daylight about the weather in Stanford, while I am looking via the internet at live pictures from a campus camera and can see that it is raining on the campus in Stanford. My utterance is made to inform John that he should take his umbrella for his way home. Thus, the relevant context can be different from the actual context of the utterance, but in any case a place and a time have to be part of the semantic content.

Germany and Poland. Furthermore, her notion of the property of being a German chancellor consists of standard information.

Table 4.1

Belief of Betty		**Content of the belief**
Notion: $N_{(\text{Willy Brandt})}$	→	the person Willy Brandt
Idea: $I_{(\text{being a German chancellor})}$	→	the property of being a German Chancellor

On the basis of this simplified version of their theory, we can illustrate their view concerning the truth-conditions. The utterance "Willy Brandt is a German chancellor" has as semantic content the proposition composed of the elements of the content expressed by the words uttered (which are at the same time the contents of the belief components), i.e. the proposition <the person Willy Brandt; the property of being a German chancellor>. As we already explained, this means that the utterance is true if Willy Brandt is a German chancellor. Let's have a look at the belief report:

(1) Betty believes that Willy Brandt is a German chancellor.

The semantic content is now enriched. It consists of a person, Betty, having a belief with the propositional content <the person Willy Brandt; the property of being a German chancellor> involving the notion n_1, i.e. Betty's notion of Brandt as the representative of Germany who symbolically went down on his knees in Warsaw.

It is important to notice that in the case of unarticulated constituents it is not only the context that determines the content (as in the case of indexicals), but also the whole situation, the word uttered, and the context. Thus a change of wording can influence the unarticulated constituent even if there is only a change of co-referential singular terms involved. Furthermore, common knowledge and mutual expectation are usually exploited in interpreting an utterance in communication.

5 Two Standard Applications: Kripke's Puzzling Pierre and Richard's Phone Booth

The details of the analysis of propositional attitudes become clear when we apply the basic idea in two important examples. The first example is Puzzling Pierre as described by Saul Kripke (1979). Suppose the Frenchman

Pierre first hears of the famous city London, but only under the French name "Londres", and that he noticed that it is described by all people as pretty. So he utters "*Londres* est jolie". We normally do not hesitate to attribute a belief to Pierre:

(10) Pierre believes that London is pretty.

To do so, we implicitly rely on principles of disquotation and translation:

Principle of Disquotation: If a normal English speaker, on reflection, sincerely assents to 'p', then he believes that p.

A principle of translation allows us to transfer the sentence "p" from one language with an adequate translation of the sentence into a different language, e.g. the French name "Londres" as part of a sentence can be translated into the English name "London" in the belief report. Let us use these principles now in Kripke's example. One day Pierre has to go to a city which is introduced to him only under the English name "London" (while he is not connecting it to the city he knows under the French name "Londres"). Visiting an ugly suburb of London, he utters the sentence "*London* n'est pas jolie". Presupposing the same principles of disquotation and translation, we have to attribute the following belief: Pierre believes that it is not the case that London is pretty. Putting both ascriptions together, we seem to end up holding that Pierre believes a contradiction (p and not-p). But according to our intuition, given the story, Pierre is a rational person, who does not have contradictory beliefs but is only lacking essential information. How can Perry and Crimmins account for these attitude reports? They claim that Pierre has two notions of London, one notion that is involving the information that it is named "Londres", that it is a famous city and that it is very pretty, etc., while the other notion involves the information that it is named "London", that it is an ugly city, etc. The first notion n_3 is based on general information transferred by testimony while the second n_4 is based on his own visual experience. The ascription

(10) "Pierre believes that London is pretty",

has two different truth-conditions: (10) is true relative to the notion n_3 if Pierre believes the content that London has the property of being pretty under the notion n_3 (involving the information about being the famous city named "Londres"). (10) is true relative to the notion n_4 if Pierre believes the content that London has the property of being pretty under the notion n_4 (involving the information about being the city he has visited named "London").

The result is that the ascription (10) is true relative to the notion $n_3$while it is false relative to the notion n_4.

This contextualization can also be found for the background principles of disquotation and translation. According to Perry and Crimmins these principles are simply wrong if one leaves out the contextual aspect. A contextualized form of disquotation could be:

> *Principle of Contextual Disquotation*: If a normal English speaker, on reflection, sincerely assents to 'p', then he believes that p *under a contextually relevant notion n.*

Before I discuss the final example, a challenge of this contextual approach can already be pointed out: How is the relevant *notion n* determined? How do we decide which one is the relevant one if Pierre has a plurality of notions (e.g. four notions)?

Another important application of the new contextualist approach is Mark Richard's story of the phone box which is a kind of the ultimate doxastic puzzle:

> "Consider A—a man stipulated to be intelligent, rational, a competent speaker of English, etc.—who both sees a women across the street, in a phone booth, and is speaking to a women through a phone. He does not realize that the women to whom he is speaking—B, to give her a name—is the women he sees. He perceives her to be in some danger—a run-away steamroller, say, is bearing down upon her phone booth. A waves at the women; he says nothing into the phone." (Richard 1983: 439)

Richard lists three sentences that we should be able to account for while they are considered as uttered by *A* watching *B* in the phone booth (while not noticing that *B* is the person he is talking to):

(11) I believe she is in danger.
(12) I believe you are in danger.
(13) The man watching you believes you are in danger.

A utters (11) to make a true report. He has a vision-based notion n_{vis} of *B* caused by his perception. *A* would, on the other hand, not sincerely assert (12) over the phone because he has no such belief of the person he is talking to. (12) involves a notion n_{phone} of *B* as the addressee of his utterance on the phone and *A* does not believe that the addressee on the phone is in danger. The additional set-up for (13) is as follows. *B* sees a man, *A*, in a building across the street waving frantically. Amused, she says (over the phone), "The man watching me believes that I'm in danger." Echoing her, *A* utters (13). According to Crimmins and Perry, *A*'s utterance of (13) is echoing *B*'s true claim, and is hence true, too.

The difference in truth-value of (11) and (12) can be explained with the same strategy we used to account for the case of Pierre. Here it is *A* who has two different notions of *B*, firstly the vision-based notion n_{vis} and secondly a notion n_{phone} as the addressee of the phone call, i.e. the person he is speaking to on the phone. According to the contextualized truth-conditions of belief reports the semantic contents of (11) and (12) are different because there are two different notions involved, though the singular proposition is the same.

Furthermore, Richard's puzzle allows us to point out an additional context-sensitivity. If we compare the utterances (12) and (13), there is only an exchange of two singular terms which are not in the scope of the belief predicate: "I" is substituted by "the man watching you". But given the epistemological situation, (12) is false while (13) is true. This is an important observation because it was the common view in philosophy of language that the exchange of singular terms is not sensitive to extensional contexts but only to intensional contexts, i.e. especially in the context of predicates expressing attitudes of believing, desiring, hoping, fearing … that …. But this example clearly illustrates "how a contextual shift can be brought about by a change in wording outside of the embedded sentence in a belief report" (Crimmins and Perry 1989b: 709).

It is interesting how Crimmins and Perry explain the phenomenon. They argue that it is produced by the use of "I". In the case of self-ascriptions of beliefs the notion of a singular term in the scope of a belief predicate is determined by the speaker's use of the singular term. Thus in (12) "you" is activating the notion n_{phone} while in (13) it is not. The relevant notion must be a different one.

6 Evaluating the Proposal

The contextualist proposal is a very promising one but it has to be developed further. Let us start with a short remark on the analysis of the difference between (12) and (13). It is not the case that this interesting observation is a consequence of the use of the word "I" in (12). Let us presuppose that A knows of himself that he is the person who has written the book "Reference and Reflexivity". Then we can produce the same effect with an utterance

(12a) "The author of the book *Reference and Reflexivity* believes that you are in danger".

Although it does not involve the use of "I", the utterance (12a) is false given the story (exactly as 12 is), because A does not believe that the addressee on the phone is in danger. We have exactly the same situation without the use of "I", namely, (12a) is false while (13) is true, and both involve in fact co-referential terms exchanged outside of the scopes of the belief predicate. So this interesting phenomenon is more general then Perry and Crimmins thought.

The second worry concerns the fact that the contextual approach includes notions of the thinker as part of the semantic content of a belief report. This is problematic because it is not always clear how the relevant notion of the thinker can be determined (if there are many notions of the same entity). Furthermore, it is worth noticing that the reporter and the listener of the belief report do usually not have a common epistemic access to the notion of the thinker. A belief report (which is not self-ascriptive) is normally used to inform a listener about the beliefs of a thinker who is different from both the reporter and the listener. Even if we ignore the problem that notions are mental particulars that only the thinker has a sufficient access to (by introspection), we still are confronted with the problem that the communicative function of the belief report is to inform a listener about the belief of a thinker and we usually are successful in doing so. But how can this be, if the semantic content essentially involves a notion of the thinker which the listener can only grasp via the reporting sentence? We are at least lacking a story that combines the general linguistic information of a belief report with a way of determining the relevant notion of the thinker the belief report is about.

Furthermore, the general strategy of unarticulated constituents is sometimes criticized as producing an implausible gap between the syntax and the semantic content (Stanley 2000 and 2002, Cappelen and Lepore 2007). This presupposes that syntax has developed just to mirror the structure of the composition of the entities involved in the semantic content. If this idea, which was introduced by the early Wittgenstein, were a fruitful background claim, it would be problematic to accept that the belief predicate is a two-place predicate and at the same expresses a three-place relation. But indexicality in general gives us good reasons to deny the Tractarian idea and to introduce new processes in determining the semantic content in addition to the syntactic structure (see Recanati 2002).

One price Perry and Crimmins have to pay—and are willing to pay—is that their semantics is no longer entirely compositional. They clearly accept that, on their view, pragmatic processes must be involved in determining the relevant notions that constitute part of the semantic content of a belief report. The recent debate in semantics is still dealing with the open question of how to draw an acceptable line between semantics and pragmatics, and the account presented here is an important contribution to this debate.

5

Situation Semantics

ISIDORA STOJANOVIC

1 Introduction

In the early 1980s, John Perry engaged in a close and fruitful colaboration with the logician Jon Barwise (1942–2000). Together, they developed a new theoretical framework known as Situation Theory. The scope of the framework was very wide, going from ontology and metaphysics, via logic, to theories of informational content, content of attitudes (such as beliefs) and of other cognitive states and faculties (such as perception), and, perhaps most importantly, theory of meaning. *Qua* theory of linguistic meaning, the framework came to be known as *situation semantics*, although the term, as used nowadays, applies to a larger class of semantic frameworks, which all have in common the use of 'situations' as a core theoretical notion (or, at least, an important technical device), but many of which, at the end of the day, do not have much else in common with the original Barwise-Perry framework.[1] The framework was laid out in "Situations and Attitudes", first

[1] For instance, the term *situation semantics* as used by contemporary semanticists will be more easily taken to refer to frameworks such as those discussed e.g. in Kratzer 2007, including Kratzer's own account (cf. Kratzer 2011), which certainly originate with the ideas put forward in Barwise and Perry (1983B), but still diverge in important ways from the Barwise-Perry framework, as much in technical details as in their failure to endorse many among the underlying philosophical ideas.

Identity, Language, and Mind: An Introduction to the Philosophy of John Perry.
Albert Newen and Raphael van Riel (eds.).

published in 1983 by MIT Press, followed by an augmented edition from CSLI Publications in 1999.[2]

It is fair to say that "Situations and Attitudes" was an extremely influential book, even if the original framework itself did not survive to become a major semantic framework in the current linguistic landscape, and even if Perry himself has abandoned it in his more recent writings. It is also fair to say that while some of the philosophical ideas underlying Perry's and Barwise's approach have been incorporated into many among the contemporary theories of content (information content, attitude content, semantic content), like, for instance, certain insights regarding the *efficiency* of language, a number of other ideas have remained ignored, misinterpreted, or simply underestimated. This may be because of a failure to recognize how deeply the approach advocated by Perry and Barwise calls into question some fundamental philosophical assumptions inherented from the Fregean tradition. In this respect, situation theory, when considered with all the bits and pieces with which it was delivered in the early 1980s, remains a largely unexplored treasure. Its founding fathers (Perry and Barwise) were probably right when they feared that situation semantics was "perhaps ahead of its time" (Barwise and Perry 1983B/1999: xxx).

My goal in this chapter is to bring to the foreground the main tenets of situation semantics. I hope that the reader will get a fair sense of the theoretical motivations that were driving the framework, and that continue to be of major significance to Perry's larger philosophical enterprise. I will thus be more concerned with the ideas themselves than with the way in which they were implemented in the formal framework of situation semantics. The chapter is organized as follows. I start by rehearsing some of the central aspects of what can be described as the *Fregean heritage*, that is, the approach pursued by Gottlob Frege (1848–1925), who is often characterized as the "father" of modern logic, semantics, and philosophy of language of the analytic tradition.[3] This will be important in order to understand the context in which situation semantics saw light, and to appreciate the almost revolutionary nature of some of the ideas behind it. Indeed, certain tenets of situation theory may be viewed as reactions directed against some of the central aspects of Frege's doctrine, which were well-established in the logi-

[2] In particular, the CSLI 1999 edition includes "Shifting Situations and Shaken Attitudes" (Barwise and Perry 1985a), written as an imaginary interview in which Barwise and Perry reply to the various comments and criticisms addressed to situation semantics.

[3] For logic, the most relevant source is Frege's "Begriffsschrift" (1879; occasionally translated in English as "Ideology"), while for language it is "Über Sinn und Bedeutung" (1892; translated in English at times as "On Sense and Denotation", at others as "On Sense and Reference").

cal, semantic, and even cognitive theories that dominated the scene in the early 1980s and which, albeit with some amendments, have persisted as the main stream up to our days. After having clarified the background, I then turn to one of the main motivations behind situation semantics (and, arguably, behind Perry's long-term project as well): the search for an account of meaning that relies upon an account of information, where the latter is crucially driven by the task of explaining how cognitive agents like us are led to *act* in ways they do, given how they are attuned to their environment. In other words, theory of meaning, theory of information, and theory of action become intertwined and even unseparable. With that in the back of our minds, I then articulate the exposition of situation semantics around eight themes:

(a) *the primacy of situations:* the idea that, both from an epistemological and a metaphysical point of view, reality consists primarily of situations, while other categories, such as individuals, properties, or locations, arise as *uniformities* across situations.

(b) *partiality:* the idea that information is, as a matter of rule rather than exception, *partial*: It tells us something only about a certain part of reality, leaving the rest open.

(c) *the efficiency of language:* the idea that the same words can be used in different contexts to mean different things (and that this, too, is a rule rather than exception).

(d) *a relational theory of meaning:* the idea that meaning should be seen as a relation between situations, rather than some kind of independent entity, detachable from both the world and the language (or other representational systems).

(e) *uniformities and constraints:* the idea is that agents get attuned to various kinds of uniformities, which allow them to classify the reality in ways that enhance their capacities for action and help them "cope with the new situations that continually arise" (Barwise and Perry 1983B/1999: 10); constraints are then seen as uniformities that arise among the ways in which situations relate to one another, while attunement to such contraints enables cognitive agents to "pick up information about one situation from another" (ibid.).

(f) *the reference relation and its relata:* an account of reference that departs from the standard account on (at least) two scores: Instead of taking reference to be a relation between a *sentence* and its *truth value*, it takes it to be a relation between *utterances* and (other) situations; secondly, instead of taking reference to be relation between a *name* (or another singular term) and an *individual*, it takes it to be a relation again between utterances (of those terms) and other situations, grounding reference on relations that hold among the individuals involved in those situations (the speaker, on the one hand, and the things and people to which/whom she is referring, on the other).

(g) *truth as a uniformity across situations:* the idea that truth is merely a device that helps us classify situations; truth partitions situations of a certain type, in particular utterance situations, in terms of a certain property that they share, viz. that there is some (appropriately related) situation that they accurately describe.

(h) *semantic innocence and attitude reports:* an account of the semantics of attitude reports, constructions such as 'believes that', 'sees' (used with 'that' or with an infinitival clause), and the like, for which one of the main motivations is that the embedded clause (i.e. the sentence that comes after 'that') should have the same meaning as it does when it occurs on its own.

Among these eight themes, five have already been singled out by Barwise and Perry in their *Preface* to the reedition issue, namely (b), (c), (d), (e), and (h) (with (c) and (d) getting merged under a single theme). I have added the other three themes, because, with hindsight, they appear to be as important and innovative as the other five. I hope that articulating situation semantics around these eight tenets will prove helpful for the exposition; but before we get there, let us first briefly describe the background from which situation theory emerged.

2 Breaking Away from the Fregean Heritage

In order to better understand the program of situation semantics, we need to remind ourselves of what the philosophical and logical landscape looked like in those times. The 1960s and 1970s were very fruitful years for the development of analytic philosophy. It was also in those years that the one of the discipline of linguistics, known today as *formal* or *model-theoretic semantics*, developed at the interface of logic and philosophy as a result of using the tools of logic to study natural language. Among the figures engaged in that sort of program let us mention Rudolf Carnap, Alonzo Church, Saul Kripke, Richard Montague, David Lewis, Jaakko Hintikka, Max Cresswell, and David Kaplan.[4] They all came from a broadly Fregean tradition, taking on board many elements constitutive of Frege's view, without questioning them.[5]

---

[4] See e.g. Carnap 1960, Cresswell 1973, Hintikka 1967, Kaplan 1989a, Kripke 1963, Lewis 1970, Montague 1970a and b (for Montague's program, see also Partee 1997).

[5] Some readers might protest against including Kripke among these authors: After all, wasn't one of his most famous contributions to philosophy of language, viz. his "Naming and

Caricaturing somewhat, here are the four foundational corners of Frege's picture:

(i) *sense* (Frege's *Sinn*): This is, figuratively speaking, the glue that serves to connect the world, the mind and the language. A linguistic expression *expresses* a sense, the mind *grasps* it, and the sense, in turn, "determines" something out there in the world. Senses themselves are not the world's citizens like the other things that surround us; rather they belong to the "Third Realm" (which is a bit like Plato's realm of ideas).

(ii) *reference* and *truth*: Sense determines reference; in particular, when the linguistic expression at stake is a sentence, it expresses what Frege calls a thought (*Gedanke*), and it has a truth value as its reference. There are two truth values, the True and the False. All true sentences share the same reference, and so do all false sentences. As Frege himself put it, at the level of reference "all that is specific is obliterated".[6]

(iii) *eternalism*: Senses are "eternal": they do not come into or go out of existence, they do not exist *in time*. Even more importantly, they do not determine reference *in time*; that is to say, a reference determined by a sense has always been, and will always be, so determined. In particular, a true sentence is atemporally true, hence it has always been and will always be true. Reference (and, in particular, truth value) is fully determined by sense. What is more, any given sentence uniquely expresses such an eternal sense. Thus if we consider the sentence "I am a philosopher" as uttered by John Perry in 2011, and the sentence "I am a philosopher" as uttered by Jon Barwise in 1991, we are led to conclude that, appearances notwithstanding, these are not the same sentence after all! Rather, they are different sentences, since context is, for Frege, a constitutive part of the linguistic expression itself.[7]

Necessity" (1972/1980), precisely an attempt to demolish Frege's view on proper names?! Though this may be right, it is fair to still see Kripke as working within a broadly Fregean tradition. Let us also note that Kripke is a pioneer of possible world semantics (indeed, his most famous contribution to logic was providing a uniform semantics for the various modal logics that, until his work, only existed as axiomatic systems), and that situation semantics was, among other things, put forward as an alternative to possible world semantics.

[6] "If now the truth value of a sentence is its reference, then on the one hand all true sentences have the same reference and so, on the other hand, do all false sentences. From this we see that in the reference of the sentence all that is specific is obliterated." (Frege 1892) Frege's choice of truth values as the reference for sentences results, at least partly, from an argument that came to be know as "the slingshot", to which we will return in Sect. 3.

[7] See e.g. Frege (1918: 332): "[T]he time of utterance is part of the expression of the thought". Among Frege scholars, there is still a lot of controversy as to what was Frege's view on context-dependence. What is fairly uncontroversial is that Frege regarded context-dependence as a flaw of natural language, and considered the latter to be defective. He wrote e.g.: "If our language were logically more perfect, we would perhaps have no further need of

(iv) *compositionality*: the idea that the meaning of a complex expression is "composed" of, or determined by, or is a function of, the meanings of its constituent expressions, given the way they are put together.[8]

It is worth pointing out another remarkable feature of Frege's view; not so much an element on its own as one that falls out from the other assumptions, more specifically from the interaction of (ii) and (iv) above: the feature sometimes called 'semantic ascent', namely, the idea that in opaque contexts, such as embedded clauses in belief reports, the reference of a sentence isn't a truth value, but rather, the customary sense of the clause at stake. Frege maintained that compositionality held not only at the level of sense, but also at the level reference, and, consequently, he maintained that if an element of a sentence is replaced by another one with the same reference, the reference of the whole sentence will remain intact. But now, consider the report "John believes that Paris is the capital of France" and replace the embedded clause with some other true sentence—which might yield, for instance, "John believes that it is sunny in Paris on April 20, 2011". While the former may be true, the latter may be false, for John may rationally believe, albeit mistakenly, that it wasn't sunny in Paris on that day. Frege's way out was to say that in such contexts, the sentence refers no longer to a truth value, but to its customary sense. Note that repeated embeddings will each time shift the reference, so that in "Mary knows that John believes that Paris is the capital of France", the embedded sentence has a meaning different both from the one it has on its own and from the one it has in "John believes that Paris is the capital of France". It is against the idea that words get to mean different things depending on how deeply they are embedded that Davidson's request for 'semantic innocence' is directed. That will be the last of the eight themes I will discuss in connection with situation semantics.[9]

As we will see in greater detail in the next section, all of these elements, except for a certain version of compositionality, were called into question and consequently rejected by the Perry-Barwise approach. Nevertheless, it may still be said that situation semantics belongs to the same broader program of model-theoretic semantics for natural language to which we alluded

---

logic, or we might read it off from the language. But we are far from being in such a position. Work in logic just is, to a large extent, a struggle with the logical defects of language" (1915: 323).

[8] How exactly compositionality is to be formulated is an open and hotly debated question in philosophy of language, which, for our purposes, we may leave open, since nothing of significance will hinge on that.

[9] On a historical note, when Perry and Barwise met, Barwise had been developing an account of constructions involving verbs of perception (like 'see') that he argued could not fit into a Fregean account of attitudes.

a couple of paragraphs ago. Barwise and Perry themselves are careful to note that "[they] want conserve ... recent insights and the powerful methods of traditional model-theoretic analysis" (1983B/1999: xii). But while situation semantics shares the aim of laying down a rigorous framework for the study of meaning in language and its relationship to cognition, it does not endorse the burden of the Fregean heritage that many other frameworks, such as those of Montague or Kaplan, have, perhaps inadvertantly, taken on board.

Already in his groundbreaking article "Frege on Demonstratives" (1977), Perry put forward serious concerns regarding Frege's theory of sense as a theory of cognitive states such as beliefs. One of the upshots of Perry's early work was to show that the Fregean notion of sense cannot at the same time accomplish the two tasks that Frege devised it for: (1) account for how mental states get to be *about* the real, concrete things that surround us; (2) account for *cognitive significance* in a way that accurately explains action and behavior. To illustrate with an example, suppose that I point to a cup and say "This cup is full of water". The first task is to account for how I can thereby express a belief about that very cup (rather than about some mental image of mine or, as Russell might have it, a sense-datum); the second is to account for how, if I am thirsty and want water, I will reach towards the cup at stake provided that I think of it as *this* cup, though I need not behave the same way if, say, I merely think that the cup from which I drank last night is full of water, without realizing that that's the cup in front of me.

The proposal that Perry outlines in those early articles (1977, 1979a) is often interpreted as a proposal to divide, as it were, Frege's notion of sense into two distinct notions:

(i) a coarse-grained notion that serves to connect the mind with the world, and to account for what our beliefs have in common when we are thinking of the same object, even though we are differently related to the object and thus think of it differently (this would be what Perry called *objects of belief*, and what Kaplan called *content*);

(ii) a finer-grained notion that serves to account for cognitive significance and its role in motivating action (this would be what Perry called *belief states*, and what Kaplan called *character*).

I believe that such an interpretation of Perry's early view is, if not outright mistaken, then certainly opposed to the spirit of Perry's approach.[10] Admittedly, it is not our task in this chapter to set straight a proper under-

[10] On a historical note, when Perry and Barwise met, Barwise had been developing an account of constructions involving verbs of perception (like 'see') that he argued could not fit into a Fregean account of attitudes.

standing of Perry's views on mind and action. But it is one of our tasks to set straight the driving motivations behind situation semantics, and one of them is clearly the aim of providing a theory of meaning (perhaps even a theory of intentionality, in Brentano's sense) that should be able to explain how agents like us can acquire and exchange information about the world around us and, as a result of that, act on this world in a way most suitable to our well-being.[11] And the first step towards such a theory lies in recognizing the extent to which Frege's appeal to senses, those third realm entities that are supposed to connect world, mind, and language, is flawed.

The picture that Perry and Barwise invite us to contemplate exploits the idea that agents get to be *attuned* to the various regularities that they encounter in their environment. Such regularities constitute *uniformities* across situations, with the help of which agents are able to classify various aspects of reality, to anticipate novel situations, and to act for the purpose of their own well-being. Among such uniformities are those that systematically relate certain situations to others. For example, whenever there is smoke, there is fire nearby. An agent who is attuned to this uniformity is better off than others who aren't, since for such an agent, a situation involving smoke carries the information that there must be fire around, and makes it possible for the agent to act appropriately (look for a fire-extinguisher, call firemen, etc.).

Uniformities across *relations* between situations are, in the Barwise-Perry terminology, *constraints*, and come in different types. For instance, the systematic connection between smoke and fire will be a nomic constraint, since it derives from the laws of physics and the causal links between fire and smoke. But constraints can also be conventional: For instance, the sound of a fire-alarm also carries the information that there is fire around. Yet, unlike the case of smoke, attunement to this constraint requires that the agent be familiar with a certain convention in place. Conventional constraints are by their very nature *conditional* on the conventions that they exploit.

Now, in this picture, meaning is merely a type of constraint—and linguistic meaning, in particular, is merely a type of conventional constraint. Thus a situation in which someone says "There is fire" carries, as before, the information that there is fire, conditional upon the conventions associated with the expressions 'there', 'is', and 'fire', and upon the assumption that the person who is saying this is a competent, sincere, and well-informed speaker.

[11] The emphasis on agents (or, as they prefer to say, *organisms*) acting for their own *well-being* is a recurrent theme in Barwise and Perry (c.f. e.g. 1983B/1999: 10 and later chapters).

Situation semantics, in a nutshell, is an attempt to provide a rigorous framework within which such a 'relational' theory of meaning may be developed and systematized.[12] While Frege and his heirs saw meaning as something out there in the "third realm" that we express through language and grasp through thought, for Perry, Barwise, and their heirs, meaning is all around us.

3 Situation Semantics: Its Tenets and Motivations

Now that we have described the philosophical context in which situation theory was born, with its constant need to question assumptions that philosophers and logicians raised in the same context pretty much took for granted, and now that we have presented, albeit in rough lines, the picture that Perry and Barwise were proposing as an alternative to the Fregean picture, let us take up one by one the eight themes listed earlier and, by elaborating on them, offer a (still rather rough) reconstrual of the framework of situation semantics.

(a) *The Primacy of Situations.* For Perry and Barwise, situations are the most basic units of reality, both from an epistemological and from a metaphysical point of view. They are epistemologically primary in the sense that, as agents, we perceive and experience, first and foremost, situations; it is only at a later stage that we experience other ontological categories, such as objects, properties, locations, or time. And they are metaphysically primary in the sense that all those other ontological categories are derived from situations, by abstracting over properties of situations and relations among them.

Now, it is a fairly common assumption, among those working in contemporary situation theory as well as those working in other frameworks, that situations have internal structure. This assumption, appearances notwithstanding, was not shared by Barwise and Perry, who insisted that, on the contrary, such a structure is imposed on situations from an external perspective, by getting attuned to similarities and uniformities across situations. Individuals, properties, relations, space-time locations, are uniformities that enable us to cluster situations together, and to classify them in various ways. Now, the widespread idea that a situation will, typically, *consist* of a number of individuals standing in various relations to one another, at a certain time and at a certain place, may indeed be traced back to

[12] The idea that meaning arises from the interaction of an agent with his or her environment was inspired, partly at least, by ideas that, at about the same time, were developed in the neighboring areas, in particular Gibson's theory of perception (see e.g. Gibson 1979) and Dretske's theory of information (Dretske 1981).

"Situations and Attitudes". But it is important to realize that the idea applies only to *abstract* situations, which are a technical device deployed by the framework, not to those situations of which reality consists and that we encounter, perceive, or act upon. As Barwise and Perry write, "we view *real* situations as metaphysically and epistemologically prior to relations, individuals, and locations. But relations, individuals, and locations are metaphysically and epistemologically prior to *abstract* situations. The latter are build out of the former as sets of various kinds" (1983B/1999: 58). Thus, the *semantic* primitives of situation semantics are individuals, relations, and space-time locations, while the primitives of the metaphysics and epistemology of situation semantics are, rather, situations themselves.

(b) *Partiality.* This core feature of situation semantics exploits the idea that information content is always partial. Consider a piece of information that tells us that Mary insulted Bill. It tells us something about Mary, and something about Bill. But it tells us nothing about Bill's mother or Mary's sister or, for that matter, anyone else in the world. Situations, by their very nature, are sources of information that give such partial information only, and are, in that respect, very different from possible worlds. A world tells us everything about everyone. If we ask whether two given objects stand in some relation, it will give us a definite answer—Yes or No. Situations, by contrast, give a definite asnwer only on a limited number of issues. For one, if the objects at stake do not even belong to the situation at stake, it is likely that the situation we are looking at won't be able to decide whether they stand in a given relation or not. But, importantly, even when the objects belong to a situation, there may be issues that the situation does not decide. It is thus possible to be have a situation in which Mary and Bill stand in the relation of insulting, but one that does not tell us *how* she insulted him—whether it was with words, with a gesture, or in some other way. The way in which the idea is cashed out is by defining situation-types in terms of *partial* functions from n-ary relations and sequences of n individuals to 0 and 1 (or to False and True). A function is *partial* (as opposed to *total*) when there are inputs on which it is undefined—which is tantamount to saying that for certain sequences of individuals, it simply doesn't tell us whether they stand in a given relation or not.

(c) *The Efficiency of Language.* The term 'efficiency' was introduced by Barwise and Perry to group together several phenomena that are tightly linked to what is nowadays preferably called 'context-dependence'. The general idea is that natural language provides means that enable the speaker to exploit various contextual factors in order to communicate information. Expressions like pronouns are a paradigmatic example of efficiency. Thus with the same linguistic device, e.g. the pronoun 'he', I can convey information about an indefinite number of individuals. If I say "He is French" in a context in which the most salient person is François, I will tell you something about François, but if I use the very same sentence in a different context, e.g. one in which we have been talking about Paul, then it is about Paul that I will say something (viz. that he is French).

For Barwise and Perry, efficiency is one of the essential properties of languages, and one that, in turn, (also) accounts for the productivity of language, i.e. the fact that with a finite vocabulary and a finite number of syntactic operations we can express infinitely many things. Note though that productivity does not coincide with efficiency. Indeed, another essential property of language that (also) accounts for productivity is compositionality, i.e. the fact that with a finite vocabulary, and a finite number of syntactic operations, we can construct infinitely many well-formed and meaningful expressions, and thereby express infinitely many things. Compositionality (which Perry and Barwise, like Frege, accept at the level of meaning, but, unlike Frege, not at the level of reference) and efficiency are complementary phenomena that together account for full productivity of language.

Efficiency itself covers a family of phenomena, just as context-dependence does, as we use the term nowadays. Pronouns such as 'he' or 'I', and adverbs such as 'here' or 'today', illustrate the sort of efficiency, or context-dependence, that is better known under the term 'indexicality', which has been widely studied and discussed in the linguistic and philosophical literature. A feature that distiguishes indexicality from other forms of efficiency is the fact that the way in which an indexical expression exploits various contextual cues is built into the expression's meaning itself. Thus it is constitutive of the meaning of the first person pronoun 'I' that it should be used for the very person who is using the pronoun (viz. the speaker). In the framework of situation semantics, this is cashed out through the way in which the interpreter exploits the constraints between utterance situations and described situations. Thus if I say "I am French", the meaning of the sentence encodes (or, if you prefer, partly consists in) the constraint that my utterance should be related to the described situation(s) by having in common that the same individual (me) should figure in both situations: in the one, in the quality of the speaker, and in the other, in the quality of the subject-matter, i.e. the individual about whom something is being said (viz. that the person is French). Although a proper discussion of the account of indexicals that one finds in situation semantics deserves a chapter of its own, the spirit of the proposal, and the idea that the meaning of indexicals deploys a certain conventional relation between the utterance and the person or object that the utterance is about, have persisted into Perry's recent theorizing about the topic (see Perry 2001B2).

As mentioned earlier, indexicality is a special case of efficiency. Two other forms of efficiency are worth mentioning. One is what is nowadays referred to as *polysemy*, namely, an essential feature of language that makes it possible for words to acquire new meanings. For example, in the past the word 'folder' used to stand for a certain class of material objects, characterized by their shape and function, but with the development of computers, it acquired a novel meaning in which it (also) stands for a certain class of electronic objects.[13]

Another form of efficiency worth mentioning is perspectival relativity, illustrated with expressions like 'behind'. Consider someone uttering "The table is behind the sofa". The informational content carried by this utterance exploits not only the constraints that come with the meaning of the sentence, but also the perspective from which the content is accessed and evaluated for truth. If the table is between me and the sofa, then from my perspective, the utterance is true, but if you are on the other side, and the sofa is between you and the table, from your perspective, the utterance is not true. Now, one could stipulate that expressions such as 'behind' privilege the speaker's perspective, in which case the perspectival relativity would work very much like indexicality, and the above utterance would be true if the sofa is between the speaker and the table. In the literature, one often finds expressions like 'behind' assimilated to indexicals. But, for one thing, perspectival expressions display a wider range of patterns than indexical pronouns. For another, perspectival relativity is an important feature not only of language, but also of the contents of beliefs and other mental states that cannot be reduced to (linguistic) indexicality.[14]

The phenomena of indexicality, polysemy, perspective-dependence, and other forms of context-dependence, and the relationships among these phenomena, are in the heart of current studies in semantics, pragmatics, and philosophy of language.[15] What matters to the present discussion is not so

---

[13] Barwise and Perry do not talk of polysemy but of ambiguity (see 1983B: 40). But I think it is helpful to put the emphasis on polysemy rather than ambiguity, since lexical ambiguity is typically accidental, while polysemy is systematic and constitutes a powerful mechanism that makes it possible to recycle the existing vocabulary in order to express new concepts. In either case, what matters is that instead of viewing ambiguity and polysemy as *defective* features of language, we see them, as Barwise and Perry write, "as another aspect of the efficiency of language. Expressions are, after all, just uniformities across certain kinds of situations, utterances. That an expression can be used in more than one way is just another feature of that expression." (ibid.)

[14] For a discussion of the perspectival relativity in thought, see Perry 1986d. See also Recanati 2007b.

[15] For collections of articles that demonstrate how large the scope of these phenomena is, see e.g. Kamp and Partee 2004 and Recanati, Stojanovic, and Villanueva 2010.

much the account that Perry and Barwise proposed of those phenomena, but rather, their recognition of all these phenomena as essential features of language that call for a rigorous analysis. Let us remind ourselves that the context in which situation semantics saw light was that of Frege's followers, and that for Frege, natural language was imperfect and defective precisely because of features such as ambiguity and context-dependence. Perry's and Barwise's insistence that these are features of *efficiency* rather than defectiveness marks an important turn in the history of semantics.

(d) *A Relational Theory of Meaning.* The idea of a *relational* theory of meaning is one of the aspects of situation semantics that remain most prominent in Perry's subsequent work, but also one that departs most strikingly from the Fregean tradition. At a first glance, one might have thought that Frege's view, too, endorses some version of a relational theory of meaning, to the extent that a sentence is *related* to a sense, or a thought, which constitutes its meaning. This is not what we mean when we speak of a *relational* theory of meaning. For Frege, meaning is an (abstract) *entity*, while sentences (of languages that we speak and in which we formulate our thoughts) are related to *it* through the relation of expressing. For Perry and Barwise, meaning *is* a certain relation, one that relates situations to situations (which, as emphasized in (a), are the basic units of reality). In the case of linguistic meaning, the relata are, on the one side, *utterance* situations, and, on the other, *described* situations (which can themselves be utterance situations, as in the case of reported discourse, such as "Mary said that it was raining").

One basic difference between situation semantics and traditional Fregean frameworks is, then, that the former sees meaning as a relation, while the latter sees it as an abstract thing or entity. There is another, related difference: The latter takes meaning to be an independent and autonomous entity; thus if there were no languages or other devices to express them, meanings would still exist. For the former, on the other hand, meaning is not really a detachable entity, since it boils down to the way in which situations relate to, and carry information about, other situations; without those very situations, the relations that hold among them and that consitute meaning would not exist either.

Let me illustrate the idea of a relational theory of meaning with an example (simplifying some aspects of the account). Suppose that I point at Paul and say "He is French". My utterance has the meaning it has in virtue of there being a relation between the utterance situation and other situations such that one and the same individual, Paul, appears in both, and that in the former, he is a salient male individual referred to by the speaker, and in the latter, he belongs among the French. Note that, given that I may be misiformed, or lying, the latter need not be real situations, but may be merely hypothetical situations in which Paul *is* French.

Let me end by briefly connecting this relational theory of meaning to the one that we find in Perry's reflexive-referential theory (Perry 2001B2). There too, meaning arises from the relations that utterances bear to the various things and events about which they convey information (or, as the case may be, *mis*information). For example, if Paul says "I am French", his utterance, we might want to say, *means* that Paul is French. In the reflexive-referential framework, the utterance gets to have such a meaning in virtue of the fact, among others, that the individual that the utterance is about (that is, Paul) stands in a certain relation to the utterance itself (viz. the relation of producing the utterance). Such relational components are explicit in what Perry calls the *reflexive* truth conditions of the utterance, and, even though they are no longer visible in what he calls the *referential* truth conditions, still, given that the latter are always derived from the former, such "incremental" levels of meaning ultimately rest upon the relations in which the utterance stands with respect to various other objects and, more generally, situations.

(e) *Uniformities and Constraints.* I have already introduced the notions of uniformity and constraint, which are central notions in situation theory, not only at the levels of language, attitudes (belief, desires, etc.), and action, but also at the level of ontology. As pointed out in the section on the Primacy of Situations, the ontological categories of individuals, properties and relations are derived from uniformities that we encounter across situations. For instance, the relation of hitting emerges merely as a regularity that we observe across all the situations that have something in common, those that with our language we would describe as involving an agent and a patient, with the former acting upon the latter in a certain way. Observing such regularities, or uniformities, and getting attuned to them, is what agents like us rely on to *classify* reality in ways that make it possible to anticipate and react to novel situations; for instance, to anticipate that, in situations of hitting in which the patient is a person (or an animal), the patient usually gets harmed, and to appropriately avoid being involved (*qua* patient) in such situations. Attunement to such uniformities, as Perry and Barwise put it, makes it possible to "cope with the new situations that continually arise", but also to "pick up information about one situation from another" (1983B/1999: 10). In the latter case, the uniformities involve two or more situations; uniformities that are themselves relational are called *constraints*.

We have already seen that constraints can be of various types, e.g. *nomic* when the constraint is based on a law of nature, as in the example of smoke meaning fire (i.e. smoke situations are constrained to be, or to appropriately involve, fire situations), but also *conventional* when the constraint is based on a convention, as in the example of the fire alarm meaning fire, and, more generally, in the case of linguistic communication. The idea is that the use of language generates uniformities across situations, and across pairs and, more generally, n-tuples of situations—in other words, constraints. Such constraints, in turn, provide language users with efficient means of conveying information, by exploiting their addressee's attunement to the constraints at stake. Suppose that I want to communicate to someone that Paul is French, in a situation in which Paul is present and I have reasons to believe that my addressee doesn't know that Paul's name is Paul. I will then likely exploit the constraint that is conventionally associated with the pronoun 'he', viz. that a situation in which an utterance of 'he' occurs constrains the described situations to be such that the individual talked about is the same as the male individual that the speaker is referring to in the utterance situation, and I will say, pointing at Paul, "He is French". Note that my utterance means that Paul is French, that is, correlates with situations in which Paul is French, only *conditionally* upon the conventions associated with the words used. The very same utterance can mean, say, that Paul works in continental philosophy, conditionally upon a different possible convention, in which 'French' would be used for continental philosophers.

Just as the relational theory of meaning is preserved in Perry's recent theorizing, so, too, are the underlying motivations behind uniformities and constraints (even if he is no longer using the same vocabulary). In particular, the idea that utterances have meaning, and convey information, only *conditionally* upon various conventions and other facts, plays a crucial role in the reflexive-referential theory. Thus even the level of *reflexive* truth conditions associated with my utterance of "He is French" hinges upon the assumption that the utterance is one of an English sentence in which the words 'he', 'is', and 'French' are used the way they are normally used: In the parlance of Perry (2001), *given* the conventions governing the use of 'he', 'is', and 'French', my utterance of '"He is French"' is true if and only if the male individual to whom I am referring with my utterance of 'he' belongs among those to whom I am referring with my utterance of 'French'. From such reflexive truth conditions, we get referential content by assuming further facts about the utterance: *Given* those conventions, and *given that* I am referring to Paul with my utterance of 'he', and to the French with my utterance of 'French', my utterance is true if and only if Paul is French. The point to be stressed is that meaning, constraints, and information more generally, are conditional upon further assumptions and facts and are, in that respect, undetachable from their contextual setting.

(f) *The Reference Relation and its Relata.* As already noted, situation semantics does not assign reference to linguistic expressions directly, the way Fregean theories and other traditional frameworks do. To be sure, even in those frameworks, due to context-dependence, reference is not assigned to indexical expressions like 'he' on their own, but rather, to pairs consisting of an expression and a context of use (or some other appropriate parameter). But even if expressions only have a reference assigned relative to a context, it is still linguistic expressions that, in those frameworks, primarily enter into the reference relation. Situation semantics rejects this idea. For one thing, it is not expressions, but particular utterances of expressions, *qua* concrete bits of reality, that can enter into the reference relation. For another, the capacity of a particular utterance of, say, 'he' to refer to a given individual, say Paul, is derived from a more basic kind of reference, in which it is the speaker using the pronoun who refers to the individual at stake. The basic status of the relations that individuals from a given situation bear with respect other individuals (possibly in other situations), in accounting for the notion of reference, is yet another way in which situation semantics departs from not only Fregean theories, but also from any view that insists on a distinction between *speaker* reference and *semantic* reference (cf. Kripke 1977).

Situation semantics also departs from the Fregean and other mainstream views when it comes to the question of what *sentences* refer to, and what their semantic values are. Since Frege, it is customary to take the semantic value (reference, extension, denotation) of sentences to be truth values. As pointed out in Section 2, Frege held that at the level of reference, "all that is specific is obliterated", and was led to the view that all true sentences have the same reference, and that so do all the false ones. In situation semantics, once again, it is not sentences (not even fully interpretted sentences, or, for that matter, propositions) that have reference. Rather, it is utterances and other concrete situations. Furthermore, what an utterance of a sentence refers to is not a truth value, but one or more (other) situations, namely, the situation(s) described by the utterance. Note that when the utterance is false, as e.g. "It rained in Paris on June 1, 2011", the described situations are counterfactual situations, rather than any real and concrete situation.[16]

[16] In the philosophical literature, there is an argument, known as the Slingshot Argument, that goes back to Frege but has been discussed and elaborated by others (such as the logician Kurt Gödel [1944]), aiming to demonstrate that sentences can only refer to truth values and cannot be consistently taken to refer to anything more specific (as would be propositions, or sets of worlds, or situations). It falls beyond the scope of this paper to explain how Barwise and Perry have resisted the argument. For discussion, see Perry 1996a.

(g) *Truth.* It may be said, in all generality, that truth is a key notion in contemporary semantics—or, at least, in model-theoretic semantics. A semantic theory assigns semantic values to expressions and, in particular, assigns values of truth and falsity to sentences. As noted previously, such values are not assigned to sentences on their own, but rather, to sequences consisting of a sentence and a certain number of other parameters, such as contexts, possible worlds, or points of evaluation more generally. It may be said, too, that while semantics deploys the notion of truth, it typically stays neutral on the *theory* of truth. In other words, values of truth and falsity are semantic primitives, on a par with other semantic primitives such as individuals or worlds, and in formal semantics the values assigned to sentences are often not the 'True' and the 'False', but numbers 1 and 0, which clearly indicates the non-committal nature of those frameworks to any theory of truth.

Now, what about situation semantics? On this score again, it departs radically from those other frameworks. For one thing, as we have already seen, the semantic values that it attaches to (utterances of) sentences are not truth values, but situations. For another, the notion of truth that one finds in situation semantics comes with a certain conception of truth, and one, moreover, that is not likely to be met with general agreement. Truth, for Barwise and Perry, is, again, just another uniformity across situations, and so is falsity. A way of explaining the idea would be to say that truth makes a partition over situations into two classes: those in which there is an utterance such that, given the constrains at play, there is one or more real situations described by the utterance, vs. the rest; while falsity, in turn, partitions situations also in two classes: those in which there is an utterance such that, given the constrains at play, there are one or more abstract, *but no real* situations described by the utterance, vs. the rest.

It takes little to see that the two partitions need not coincide, since situations in which there is no utterance (or at least none that is interpretable) will count among "the rest" on either partition. More importantly, just as constraints are often *conditional* upon conventions and assumptions of various sorts, truth and falsity too are uniformities that will be conditional on other things and, in particular, on the constraints in which the situation at stake is involved. Thus consider again the example of an utterance of "There is fire", made in a situation in which there is indeed fire. This utterance situation may be classified under the truth-uniformity, *conditional upon* the conventions associated with the words 'there', 'is', and 'fire'. Yet the very same situation may be classified under the falsity-uniformity, conditional upon another possible convention, such as one that would associate the word 'fire' with, say, situations in which it is sunny, if in fact it is *not* sunny in that situation.

To bring the point home, when it comes to truth, we see again a considerable departure not only from Frege's own approach, but also from assumptions and, one could even say, *practices* shared by a majority of existing frameworks. Within those frameworks, truth is a primitive notion. Furthermore, the question of what are the primary bearers of truth is seen as substantive, and it is often taken for granted that it is propositions, or contents, that bear a truth value, and to which the truth predicate primarily applies. For Barwise and Perry, on the other hand, truth is derivative: It is just a regularity to which agents get attuned that helps them classify reality and retrieve information in ways useful in anticipating novel situations and planning action. The question of what are the primary bearers of truth value becomes ill-conceived, and to the extent that it has an answer, it is situations that are susceptible of being true or false. There is thus nothing special about truth: Simply, situations can be classified as true or false, just as they can be classified as, e.g. evening situations, situations of hitting, or situations 2km north of London. Of course, an agent's capacity to classify a given situation as true rather than false can prove particularly useful; but so can an agent's capacity to classify a given situation as dangerous rather than harmless. Just as danger falls out as a uniformity across situations, to which agents get attuned, and which they can exploit in acting for their own well-being, so do truth and falsehood.

(h) *Semantic Innocence and Attitude Reports.* To close this presentation of situation semantics, let me turn to a particular application of the framework, namely to *attitude reports* (broadly speaking), such as "John believes that Mary used his car", but also reports involving verbs of perception, such as "John saw that Mary used his car" or even "John saw Mary use his car". As we have seen, Frege's own approach was particularly implausible when it came to accounting for attitude reports, for he assumed compositionality at the level of reference and, given that sentences that merely coincide in their truth value cannot be safely substituted for one another within attitude reports, was led to the view that, in such contexts, sentences have as their reference not a truth value, but what would have been their sense if they were not embedded. Even though this feature of Frege's view did not survive to the present days, it is still true that broadly Fregean frameworks have difficulties when it comes to attitude reports. Now, it is beyond the aim of this chapter to present Perry and Barwise's semantics of attitude reports, so let me simply point out some features of their framework that make it superior both to Fregean frameworks and to frameworks that rely on possible world semantics (such as the one developed by Jaakko Hintikka). As pointed out previously, the semantic values that situation semantics associates with sentences are not truth values, nor are they senses, propositions, or sets of possible worlds, but rather, situations. An attitude report of the form '*A Vs* (that) *S*' (where *A* is a singular term, *V* a verb of attitude or perception, and *S* a sentence) requires that the agent *A* stands in relation *V* to the situation(s) to which *S* makes reference. Thus whether a sentence occurs on its own or as a 'that'-clause in an attitude report (however deeply embedded) does not impinge on the sentence's meaning; in either case, its reference (in the sense discussed in Section (f) above) will consist of one or more situations, which is what makes it possible for Barwise and Perry to preserve our "semantic innocence" (to use the phrase Davidson aptly coined). Now, it should be noted, too, that situation semantics, although "semantically innocent", rejects nevertheless compositionality at the level of reference. Thus there can be attitude reports of the form '*A Vs* that *S*' and '*A Vs* that *S**' in which *S* and *S** happen to refer to the same situations yet the one report is true but not the other; the standard Hesperus-Phosphorus cases fall into this category. However, in *direct* perception reports, sentences referring to the same situations may be substituted for one another *salva veritate*. Thus suppose that Mary is Mrs. Jones, but that John is confused and thinks that "Mrs. Jones" is someone other than Mary. Then "John believes that Mary used his car" may be true without "John believes that Mrs. Jones used his car" being *ipso facto* true. On the other hand, if "John saw Mary use his car" is true, then "John saw Mrs. Jones use his car" will also be true.

As a final remark, let me point out a way in which situation semantics of attitude reports is also superior to the frameworks inspired by Kripke's possible worlds semantics for modal logics. Such frameworks are known as Hintikka-style semantics (cf. Hintikka 1962), or as doxastic-epistemic logics. In those frameworks, '*A* believes that *S*' is true iff *S* is true in all the worlds that *A* takes to be possible (or, as it is customary to speak, iff *S* is true in all of *A*'s doxastic alternatives for the actual world); similarly, '*A* knows that *S*' is true iff *S* is true in all the worlds that are, from *A's* perspective, indistinguishable from the actual world. Such possible world frameworks face the so-called problem of logical omniscience. Consider something that is a truth of logic or mathematics. Since such truths hold in all possible worlds, *ergo* in all of the doxastic alternatives of a given agent as well, Hintikka-style semantics is committed to the view that it is true to report that the agent *believes* a given truth, which goes against intuitions. There are many logical and mathematical truths that we fail to know and fail to believe. Situation semantics has some advantages in this respect, too, for any logical or mathematical sentence will, just like any other sentence, have as its reference one or more situations, and if the agent at stake is not appropriately related to those situations, the belief report may come out false, as expected. For reasons of space, I must abstain from discussing the issue of what sort of situations mathematical sentences describe, but let us simply consider what seems to be a fairly trivial truth of logic, such as "Paula used John's car or she didn't use his car". Suppose furthermore that John has no idea who Paula is, and has no connection to her. Then, in situation semantics, the report that John believes that very truth need not come out as true. For that report to be true, John would need to be related to either a situation in which Paula used his car or to one in which she didn't, hence on either option, to a situation that involves Paula, which, by hypothesis, isn't the case.

What I have tried to do in this chapter is to offer a survey of situation semantics, by developing it around the above eight themes. I hope to have shown to what a large extent situation theory was an ambitious program that departed from the mainstream approaches in radical ways. While the pioneering work of Barwise and Perry was extremely influential, it is also fair to say, with the hindsight, that situation semantics did not become a widely pursued program, and that its contemporary off-springs (such as Kratzer's semantics) come much closer to the mainstream views than does the original Barwise-Perry framework. Now, my aim in this chapter was not so much to present situation semantics in all the details of its sophisticated machinery, but rather, to dwell more on the underlying philosophical ideas, among which there are several that, as I tried to show, continue to occupy a central place in John Perry's long-term philosophical enterprise.[17]

Acknowledgements

I would like to thank Raphael van Riel and Albert Newen for their invitation to contribute to the present volume and for their helpful comments, and Neil Van Leeuwen for suggesting me as a contributor. On a personal note, I would like to express my immense gratitude to John Perry. Finally, let me acknowledge participation and partial funding from the following projects: "Semantic Content and Context-Dependence", MICINN, Spanish Government, grant n° CSD2009-0056; "Context, Content and Compositionality", European Community's Seventh Framework Programme (FP7/2007-2013), grant n° 229 441–CCC, and "Perspectival Thoughts and Facts" (PETAF), EC-FP7/2007-2013, grant n° 238 128.

[17] For other helpful surveys of situation semantics and its impact on contemporary semantics, see e.g. Kratzer (2007) or Ginzburg (2011).

Part Two

Persons and Their Minds

6

Perry on Self-Knowledge

NEIL VAN LEEUWEN

1 Problems of Self-Representation

A man is looking out the large window at planes on the tarmac. The PA system announces, "John Perry to the counter at Gate 27A." The sound waves strike the man's eardrums and are translated into neural impulses. His brain signals his leg muscles, which contract and carry him to the counter. He speaks, "*I* am John Perry."

The man must believe that *he* is John Perry. This is a clear case of self-belief, which is self-knowledge when it is true, justified, and whatever else is needed for knowledge.[1]

But what is self-belief? The intuitive answer is: Self-belief is just belief about an individual, where that individual is the same person as the person who has the belief. But this answer is insufficient.

To see the insufficiency, let's fictionally alter our initial example. *a-John*, as I'll call him, is an amnesiac version of John Perry. a-John is sitting in the airport and has forgotten he is John Perry. Hearing the announcement, a-John forms the belief that *John Perry should go to the counter at Gate 27A*. Yet a-John remains sitting. Due to amnesia, he doesn't know or believe that he is John Perry.

Could we rectify the situation just by giving him more information about who John Perry is? Say someone, attempting to help, stopped and told

[1] This is a broader sense of self-knowledge than the sense in which self-knowledge refers only to knowledge of one's own mental states. I explain the relation between those senses in the next section.

Identity, Language, and Mind: An Introduction to the Philosophy of John Perry.
Albert Newen and Raphael van Riel (eds.).

him that John Perry is a philosopher with a white beard, who happens to be sitting near 27A. a-John could then go on to infer *the philosopher with a white beard near 27A should go to the counter*. But he still doesn't stand up, because he doesn't realize he is that philosopher.

We can now see why the intuitive characterization of self-belief is insufficient. a-John has a belief about an individual—that that individual should go to the counter—and the individual that belief is about is the same as the individual who has the belief (a-John/John Perry). Yet this still isn't self-belief, which is why he is unmoved.

Our problem is thus clear. We need to sufficiently characterize self-belief.

a-John does of course have self-beliefs. He believes he is sitting down; he believes he is in an airport; he believes he is wearing shoes; he believes he feels warm; he believes he'd like to smoke a pipe. So we need to say how these genuine self-beliefs differ from the beliefs that, although they're about him, are not self-beliefs.

a-John has three notions in his mind that are *of* him, which I notate[2] as follows:

[John Perry]
[white-bearded philosopher near 27A]
{self-notion}

Each of these notions figures as a constituent in beliefs a-John has, but it would seem the genuine self-beliefs employ the self-notion. For example:

{self-notion} am [in an airport]

So we can say: Self-belief is just belief about an individual, where that individual is the same person as the person who has the belief, *and* the individual is represented in the belief by the self-notion.

Have we solved our problem? Not yet, for even though the claim just made is true, an analogous problem arises at the level of notions, which are ways of thinking about something. The intuitive characterization of self-notions is this: A self-notion is a notion about an individual, where the individual who has the notion and the individual it is about are the same. But this is insufficient, since a-John's notions [John Perry] and [white-bearded philosopher near 27A] both satisfy the intuitive characterization, without being the self-notion. When a-John thinks *John Perry*, he's thinking about himself without knowing it, so the [John Perry] notion is *not* the self-notion.

[2] I'll clarify the difference in meaning between the square and curly brackets shortly.

We haven't solved the initial problem of self-belief, but we've sharpened it. We now need to give a theory of what a self-notion is. The plan for the rest of the paper is to use John Perry's (the real-life philosopher's!) ideas to do just that.

2 The Plan: Introducing Perry on Self-Knowledge

A central theme in Perry's philosophy is that there are often many different ways to think (or talk or write) about the same thing. Understanding the different ways systematically is critical to understanding cognition and communication. Developing this theme as it applies to thinking about the self, I structure this paper around three questions.

> *First*, how should we classify the different ways of having information about the self? There are several ways I can receive and retain information about me. What are the ways?
>
> *Second*, how does self-knowledge fit in with the structure of knowledge, belief, and cognition, in general?
>
> *Third*, how can we characterize the self-notion, using the general picture of knowledge, belief and information retention at our disposal?

Answering the second question is crucial to answering the third. To see why, let's return to our example of a-John, whom we'll leave behind entirely after this section. By analyzing how a-John can come to realize who he is, we can start to see what it is for a notion to be a *self*-notion.

There a-John sits, accumulating information. Some information he accumulates is tied to the name "John Perry". a-John looks in the bag next to him and sees a book on the philosophy of John Perry, with a picture of a man with a white beard on it. He learns Perry is a philosopher of language with a white beard.

But other information he acquires is immediately cognized as being about himself. Touching his chin, he realizes that *he* has a beard. Seeing his reflection in the window, he learns his beard is white.[3] Looking around he sees *he* is in an airport at gate 27A. Thinking rather deep philosophical thoughts about language, he realizes that *he* is a philosopher of language.

Suddenly, a light bulb goes on. He exclaims, "I am John Perry!"

What just happened?

---

[3] Of course, seeing one's reflection only feeds information into the self-notion file if one realizes it is a reflection, as *a-John* does in this case. We'll see Perry's treatment of the Ernst Mach example below, in which Mach didn't realize he was seeing a reflection. In that case, the reflection-generated percepts (initially) don't feed into the self-notion file.

There are (at least) two kinds of information channel active in a-John's pre-realization state. a-John's realization occurs when the two channels become connected in the right way.

Channel 1. On the one hand, a-John sees big signs with symbols like

27A

which are encoded in perceptual states. He also feels a seat underneath him and sees the airplanes outside the window. This inflow of information is from his immediate environment and his own body and relates that environment and body to *him*. For example, his 27A percept represents the sign as being a certain distance away, and although he's not thinking of himself in having that percept, *he* is the entity from whom the 27A sign appears as being that certain distance away. So—this is the critical point—the 27A percept (along with a host of others like it) is guaranteed to convey information that is at least in part about him: It locates him in an environment. Let's call this kind of information *agent-relative*, since the informational content always relates the agent receiving the information to a surrounding environment. The agent receiving the information is *identical* with the agent *to whom* the inflowing information relates the environment. Even amnesiacs can use the agent-relative information flow to form self-beliefs, with reflexive contents like *I am in an airport*. (Note to the reader: I use curly brackets "{...}" to designate notions in the mind that derive from this agent-relative information channel.)

Channel 2. On the other hand, some of the information a-John receives is not relative to him at all—at least not until he finds a way to connect it to himself. He might read that interest rates have gone up in Singapore, that on right triangles $a^2 + b^2 = c^2$, or (crucially) that John Perry is a philosopher. This kind of information we can call *objective* (or *detached*, for reasons that become clear), since the information gleaned from this flow isn't without further realization taken to relate to the agent him- or herself.[4] (Note to the reader: I use square brackets "[...]" to designate notions in the mind that are associated with objective information.)[5]

4 It happens to be the case that objective information flow is always carried by a channel of agent-relative information flow. For example, learning the objective information *that there is coffee in Colombia* requires being in a perceptual state: either of seeing the assembly of letters "there is coffee in Colombia", or of hearing that sentence spoken, or of being in Colombia and seeing coffee beans. But assume for now that we can separate out the objective portion of the channel.

5 This use of the phrases "agent-relative", "objective", and "detached" comes from Perry's own work; but the use of the curly and square brackets to designate notions associated with either agent-relative or objective information is my own convention.

When a-John realizes *he* is John Perry, he must be noticing that there is simply too much coincidence between the information from the objective flow about John Perry and the information from the agent-relative flow about himself and his place in his environment. Both he and Perry have white beards, think philosophical thoughts, have something to do with gate 27A, etc.

When a-John realizes *I am John Perry*, he is thinking something like:

> {the individual seeing 27A, feeling the bench, hearing the PA …} am [the philosopher named John Perry, a man with a white beard, a man who must come to 27A …]

Otherwise put:

> {self-notion} am [John Perry notion]

What this suggests is that the self-notion is constitutively linked to agent-relative information—in a way that has yet to be explained. Furthermore, a-John has his realization *by* linking the objective information about John Perry *to* the self-notion and agent-relative information. In short, the suggestion is, roughly, that {the individual seeing 27A, feeling the bench beneath, hearing the PA announcement …} *is* a-John's self-notion. As Perry writes: "[S]elf-notions are those that have the special role of being the repository for information gained in normally self-informative ways and the motivator for actions done in normally self-effecting ways" (Perry 2002c: 205). I call this *Perry's Thesis*.

It will take work to flesh out this thesis, but the discussion so far already gives an idea of Perry's methodology. First (in order of logical priority), he distinguishes different kinds of information channel or "ways of knowing", including ways of knowing that for "architectural" reasons give information about the person using them; second, Perry also distinguishes different classes of action, including what he calls "normally self-effecting ways of acting"; third, he uses the ways of knowing and categories of action to implicitly define the self-notion, as standing in certain relations to those ways and categories (this strategy is essentially functionalist); fourth, self-belief (and hence self-knowledge) can be explained by appeal to the self-notion.

3 Question 1: What Are the Different Ways of Having Information About the Self?

The phrase "self-knowledge" often refers specifically to knowledge of one's own mental states. But Perry's use of the phrase is broader and, in a sense, more fundamental. Perry generally uses "self-knowledge" to mean any knowledge one has of one's self, where that knowledge has the self-notion as a constituent: knowledge one might express using "I" or "me". So my knowing I'm wearing a blue shirt is self-knowledge in this extended, Perryan sense. Importantly, however, my knowing that the tallest philosopher at University of Johannesburg is wearing a blue shirt would *not* count as self-knowledge, even if I am he, so long as I don't realize that I am he.

Any self-knowledge in the more restricted sense of knowledge about one's mental states (assuming one has that knowledge "from the inside") will be self-knowledge in Perry's sense, which is why Perry's sense is broader. But it's also fair to say that understanding self-knowledge in Perry's sense is required for complete understanding (if such is possible) of self-knowledge in the more limited sense. Suppose a psychotherapist tells me that the tallest philosopher at University of Johannesburg is anxious. This could be knowledge of one of my mental states without properly being self-knowledge, because unless I realize that I am the person so described, I won't really know that *I* am anxious. So, importantly, addressing Perry's concerns is crucial to addressing the more restricted concern of self-knowledge of mental states that has so gripped the philosophical community.

Let's see how Perry classifies the different ways of having knowledge about oneself.

In "Myself and *I*," Perry distinguishes three ways one could have information about—or in some sense "know" about—oneself (Perry 1998c).

1: agent-relative knowledge
2: self-attached knowledge
3: knowledge of the person one happens to be

In the next subsections, I'll explain all three of these. It will turn out that only self-attached knowledge (2) is self-knowledge in the sense we're looking for. But understanding the other senses is required for understanding this one.

Agent-Relative Knowledge (1)

At the beginning of "Thought without Representation," Perry writes:

> I see a cup of coffee in front of me. I reach out, pick it up, and drink from it. I must then have learned how far the cup was *from me*, and in what direction, for it is the position of the cup relative to me, and not its absolute position, that determines how I need to move my arm. But how can this be? I am not in the field of vision: no component of my visual experience is a perception of me. (Perry 1986d: 171, Perry's italics)

This passage describes agent-relative knowledge, which requires "no concept or idea of oneself" (172), even though the information it encodes is partly about the self.

To put it another way: Although visual percepts encode information that is in some sense about oneself—e.g., I have a computer screen in front of *me*—the *self* finds no articulation in those percepts. The seen computer screen is articulated by shape, color, and distance. The wall behind it is similarly articulated. But where is the *self* in the visual percept? Nowhere! Nevertheless, that percept locates the self in his/her environment.

Agent-relative knowledge is the kind of "self-knowledge"[6] that's available to a cat, even though (we assume) cats have no *concept* of the self. When a cat sees a mouse before her, she knows how far to pounce, which means her visual percepts convey how far the mouse is from *her*. We can see this by considering two other proposals for the informational content of the cat's visual perception of the mouse's location. One might say that the cat just sees *where* the mouse is—not in relation to her—simply *where* the mouse is.[7] But unless this "where" is related to the cat, how does she know how far to pounce? The cat has no representation of absolute space, and hence has no representation of herself or the mouse in it. Rather, the cat must see the space around her relation to *her*. A more tempting (but still wrong) proposal is that the cat sees the mouse *only* as spatially related to the environment they are both in—say, as being in a location in the room. Although better, this proposal also fails. For the cat sees the mouse differently depending on where *she* (the cat) is, even if the mouse is in the same spot in the room; the mouse takes up more of the cat's visual field when she is closer to it. It follows that the cat's percepts of the mouse don't just carry information about where the mouse is in the room; they also carry information about how far the mouse is from *her*. Thus, by the same token, they carry information about how far *she* is from the mouse, even though she in no way sees herself. These same points, I believe, would generalize to many other species.[8] In sum, agent-relative knowledge relates one's environment

---

[6] The scare quotes here indicate that this way of having information falls short of self-knowledge in the classic Perryan sense, in which the self is represented or articulated by the self-notion.

[7] This suggestion is of course simplistic. But I did hear it made at a professional philosophy conference.

[8] Yet this humble form of self-knowledge is also critical to all *human* action. Why "all"? The reason is that: "However complex our lives are, everything we do comes down to performing operations on the objects around us—objects in front of us, behind us, above us; objects we are holding; objects we can see" (Perry 1998c: 326–7). Even when I write an email to someone 8,000 kilometers away, I must be aware of how far the keyboard is from me, which requires agent-relative knowledge. Furthermore, many (most?) actions even bypass more sophisticated

to oneself (conversely, oneself to one's environment), without the self's being an articulated constituent of the representations in which the knowledge consists.

But that's not all agent-relative knowledge does. Much agent-relative knowledge consists of information about the relation between the agent and some external object, as I just described. But—crucially—much agent-relative knowledge is *just* about the agent. This tight feeling conveys to me that my shoulder is tense. Just as the notion of *me* is not a constituent of the cat's mouse perception, so the notion of *me* is not a constituent of the shoulder pain. In Perry's terms, there are many "agent-relative roles"[9] occupied by objects in our environment—the keyboard is in the *thing-my-fingers-are-touching* role—and objects in agent-relative roles are sources of agent-relative knowledge.[10] Importantly, one logical relation that defines an agent-relative role is *identity*, in which case the occupant of the role is identical to the receiver of the information.

Thus, an important sub-class of agent-relative knowledge is acquired through what Perry calls "normally self-informative ways of knowing". Pleasures, pains, the feeling of bodily postures, and other sensations are all normally self-informative ways of knowing. They are architecturally guaranteed—guaranteed by the way the organism is set up—to carry information about the agent to the *same* agent, even though the agent him/herself is not an articulated constituent of the representational vehicle of that information. The important feature of this class of agent-relative knowledge that follows from this is that the agent can't be wrong about whom it is about. I can be wrong about whom I see when I see you, but I can't be wrong about whose shoulder hurts when my shoulder hurts. Following Shoemaker, Perry

---

forms of self-knowledge. People often pick up coffee cups and drink without deciding to do so on each act of picking up; rather, having decided to drink already, their bodily movements are adjusted by the varying agent-relative knowledge coming in through visual, proprioceptive, and olfactory faculties.

[9] Perry introduces this phrasing in his "Self-Notions" (1990c). That essay also introduces the phrases "normally self-informative ways of knowing" and "normally self-effecting ways of acting".

[10] In "Myself and I", Perry distinguishes between basic and derived agent-relative roles. Basic agent-relative roles are defined by relations between agents and things in their nearby environments. My chair is in a basic agent-relative role in relation to me, the thing-I'm-on role. Derived agent-relative roles are occupied by things more distant that relate to us *via* the occupants of basic agent-relative roles. Perry's example is that Bill Clinton is the occupant of the person-I'm-watching role, but this is derived, since the TV must first be in the thing-I'm-watching role. In this paper, since I only talk about basic agent-relative roles, that's what "agent-relative role" refers to in all cases here.

calls this kind of information "immune to error through misidentification".[11]

Why is immunity to error through misidentification so important? It's what enables normally self-informative ways of knowing to ground the self-notion, which is an essential constituent of self-knowledge in the more robust sense, which Perry calls "self-attached knowledge". I explain how this works in the penultimate section. Now let's turn to classifying the other two forms of knowing about the self.

Self-Attached Knowledge (2) and Knowledge of the Person One Happens to be (3)

Why the term "attached"[12] in "self-attached knowledge"? The short answer is that this kind of self-knowledge is attached to the self-notion.

> Ordinarily all one's knowledge about oneself is integrated around a special sort of idea or notion of oneself that we express with "I." While my perception that the beer is in front of me may not require a representation of myself, the information I acquire is immediately integrated into self-attached knowledge, that I might express with "I see beer" or "there is a beer in front of me." And when I read a piece of email that says that John Perry's paper is overdue, I integrate this information into self-attached knowledge, "My paper is overdue," and I realize that it is me that has to get to work. (Perry 1998c: 333)

We can see the importance of the self-notion by looking at two examples that highlight the difference between self-attached knowledge (2), which deploys the self-notion, and knowledge of the person one happens to be (3), which doesn't. The first example is one of Perry's favorites (with help from Ernst Mach), and the second example is mine (with help from Victor Hugo). In each example, the agent starts with knowledge of the person he happens to be, without having self-attached knowledge.

Example 1: Ernst Mach reports that he stepped onto a bus one day and saw a shabby pedagogue at the other end, a man with rumpled clothing and very academic looking (Mach 1914). He thought *that man is a shabby pedagogue*.

---

[11] Sensations of phantom limbs are not a counterexample here. The phantom limb sensation is of something that doesn't exist, but the agent still can't be wrong about whose phantom limb it is. Remember, in "immunity to error through misidentification" it's the *who* (yourself) you can't be wrong about, even though you might be wrong about what it is you sense. Another example (from Perry), on feeling flushed, you might wrongly think you're blushing, but you still can't be wrong about who's feeling flushed.

[12] Note to the reader: The terms "linked" and "attached" have a special meaning for Perry, which I clarify in view of his broader cognitive picture in the section called "Question 3".

Example 2: Jean Valjean is in prison and hears the announcement "24601 will be put in solitary confinement." He thinks *24601 is unfortunate*.[13]

Mach's thought doesn't motivate him to improve his appearance, and Valjean's thought doesn't cause him dread. Yet Mach was just seeing himself in a mirror at the end of the bus, and 24601 is the prison number of Jean Valjean.

Mach and Valjean both had knowledge about themselves without realizing it, which is exactly what Perry calls "knowledge of the person one happens to be". Mach, in some sense, should have been motivated to tidy up, while Valjean should have felt dread. But they didn't, and the problem is a failure of realization. Generally, knowledge of the person one happens to be consists of information about oneself, in which the notion that is *of* the person in question is not the self-notion and is not linked to it either.

To have the needed realization, Mach would have to have a thought that predicates being the man he sees of *himself*, a thought which would involve his self-notion. Similarly, Valjean would have to have a thought that predicates being 24601 of himself. But the sources of images in the mirror are not always clear, even when it's *you*, and numbers used as names are easy to forget, even when it's your number. So not all knowledge about oneself is self-attached.

To attain genuinely self-attached knowledge, Mach and Valjean would have to have thoughts with these structures:

{self-notion} am [man appearing at the opposite end of the bus]
{self-notion} am [24601]

This makes clear why we need an account of the self-notion, for without this we can't make sense of the above thoughts, and those thoughts just are instances of self-knowledge in the required sense. But providing such an account is tricky. One might say that the self-notion is just a notion that refers to the self. But in Valjean's case, [24601] is a notion that refers to Valjean's self, but it's not his self-notion. So the phrase "a notion that refers to the self" won't do as a definition of *self-notion*. Alternately, one might say that the self-notion is the notion one expresses with the word "I". That's true, but not explanatory. In particular, it doesn't tell us why, prior to Valjean's realization, he expresses {self-notion} with "I" but not [24601].[14] And to understand why, we need an account of the self-notion.

---

[13] This is not actually an episode from *Les Miserables*; rather, it's inspired by the combination of my reading Perry and listening to musical theatre.

[14] An interesting question that arises here, although I don't have space for it, is the following. If Valjean both believes *I am not going to solitary* and believes *24601 is going to solitary*,

So explaining the self-notion is still needed. To wrap up this section, this chart summarizes key features of the three forms of self-knowledge.

Table 6.1

	Agent-relative knowledge	**Self-attached knowledge**	**Knowledge of the person one happens to be**
Conceptual structure	Lacks a constituent for the self (i.e. no self-notion), but informationally relates the surrounding environment and the agent him/herself to the agent	Uses the self-notion in predicating a property of oneself (e.g. {self-notion} am *writing a paper on self-notions*)	Uses a notion that, unbeknownst to oneself, refers to oneself (e.g. [24601] *is headed to solitary*)
Form of verbal expression	Will often lack any constituent that refers to the self (e.g. "There's the cup!")	Uses first-person indexicals like "I" (e.g. "I am writing a paper.")	Uses third-personal name or description ("24601 is going to solitary.")
Relation to action	Required for guiding behavior in relation to the immediate environment (e.g. one's cup percepts when one is grabbing the cup)	Used in practical reasoning and decision making, which issues in action (e.g. I desire that {self-notion} *finish writing*; I believe *coffee helps writing*; action consequence: I get more coffee.)	Often mere verbal expression or heuristic behavior (finding out who); cannot be used in ways that treats the subject of the knowledge as the agent (e.g. Valjean won't try to escape *his* solitary confinement on learning of 24601's.).

has he believed a contradiction? The question is of course analogous to Kripke's famous Pierre case, where Pierre believes *Londres est beaux* but also *London is not beautiful*. Perry's solution to that problem, which can be extended to the present case, is found in his "Reference and Reflexivity" (2001B2).

4 Question 2: How Does Self-Knowledge Fit in with the Structure of Knowledge in General?

Understanding the elusive self-notion is critical to understanding self-knowledge. But to understand the self-notion, we must first understand Perry's view of ideas, notions, files, and beliefs in general. In "Knowledge, Possibility, and Consciousness," Perry describes the structure of belief and knowledge with the metaphor of a building.

> Think of the architecture of our beliefs as a three-story building. At the top level are detached files (ideas associated with notions). ... At the bottom level are perceptions and perceptual buffers. Buffers are new notions associated with the perceptions and used to temporarily store ideas we gain from the perceptions until we can identify the individual, or form a permanent detached notion for him, or forget about him.
>
> The middle level is full of informational wiring. Sockets dangle down from above, and plugs stick up from below. The ideas in the first floor perceptual buffers and in the third-floor files are constantly compared. When there is a high probability that they are of a single person or thing, recognition (or misrecognition) occurs. The plug from the buffer is plugged into the socket for the notion. Information then flows both ways.
>
> The information flowing up from the perception adds new ideas to the file associated with the notion. ... The information flowing down to the bottom level enriches the perceptual buffer and guides my action toward the objects I see and hear in ways that would not be supported just by the ideas picked up from perception. (Perry 2001B2: 120–1)

One central idea of this passage is that the objective knowledge on the top floor needs to be connected to the perceptual information on the bottom floor in order for that objective information to be usable in action. In other words, *I* can't use objective information unless it's attached to something or other on the bottom floor. This gives a clear idea of where to look for the self-notion: the bottom floor. Let's parse a few of the terms Perry introduces.

Constituents of thought, for Perry, are mental entities that can be distinguished by the type of reference they have. Constituents of thought that represent general properties and relations, like the property *being red* or the relation *being a brother of*, are *ideas*; constituents of thought that represent particular things, like *Barry Sanders' garage* are *notions*. A *file* is just Perry's way of talking about the collection of information associated with one's notion of a particular thing. So my file for *Barry Sanders' garage* will have the idea *red* in it if, and only if, I believe that Barry Sanders' garage is red.[15] If I come to believe Barry Sanders has painted his garage, my file

[15] What if I merely imagine Barry Sanders' garage is red, without having a belief on the matter either way? Will I then still have the idea *red* in my file for Sanders' garage? That issue

may then update to have the idea *blue* in it. Finally, a *perceptual buffer* is just a first-story notion/file that tracks information about an object (it could be oneself) through one or more perceptual channels.[16]

What is remarkable about human cognition is that one can have a notion/file of Barry Sanders' garage, without ever having seen it. I may just have read about it in the "Almanac of Detroit Lions Greats" and formed my notion and beliefs solely on that basis. If so, I could find myself in a curious situation: walking through Sanders' neighborhood, I may see the garage, without knowing it's the garage I have beliefs about. On seeing it, I form a perceptual buffer for the garage, which starts to accumulate perceptions and ideas: *pretty*, *red*, *rectangular*, *has room for three cars*, *has a running back in it*, and so on. I then notice a high degree of coincidence between my third-story "detached" file for Barry Sanders' garage, which I formed on reading the "Almanac", and my first-story perceptual buffer.

The moment I say "Aha! That's Barry Sanders' garage!" is the moment, to continue Perry's metaphor, when the plug sticking up from the garage perceptual buffer connects with the socket dangling down from the Barry Sanders' garage file on the third floor. We can notate the structure of my thought as follows (where subscripts indicate: cognitive structure/information source):

$$\{\text{This}_{\text{VisualBuffer/Garage}}\}\text{ is [Barry Sanders' Garage}_{\text{ThirdStoryFile/Almanac}}]$$

Once this judgment is reached, my file [Barry Sanders' Garage$_{\text{ThirdStory-File/Almanac}}$] is *attached*; it's linked to—and temporarily contains the contents of—the particular perceptual buffer that I am using to track the garage before me. When I leave Sanders' neighborhood, I'll still have the third-story file, but it won't be attached to any buffer. The file will have been modified to include some things I learned from visual experience. So the file will now have the structure [Barry Sanders' Garage$_{\text{ThirdStoryFile/Almanac\&Vision}}$]. What's the point of having detached files? First, you wouldn't want to *forget* what you learned. And second, having a detached file, if its information is largely accurate, is useful in shaping anticipations of objects for when one actually encounters them. For example, if I had read in the "Almanac" that Sanders keeps a ferret in his garage, and if I am allergic to ferrets, I'll know to keep my distance, even if the ferret hasn't made its way into my perceptual

lies outside this paper. But my own view—not Perry's—is that the idea *red* would still be in the file, just with an imaginative (non-belief) attitude valence.

[16] Places Perry introduces this terminology: Perry 2001B1: 50 and 1998c: 325.

buffer.[17] Detached files can become attached and thereby make their contents useful.

We can already see that the self-notion must be a first-floor notion, but one that in different forms of self-knowledge attaches to files on the third floor. *I* am the entity that perceives and does things in my immediate environment (using first floor information). *Neil Van Leeuwen* is an entity whose name appears on an airplane ticket and is represented in an electronic airline database (third floor information). So knowing the identity that *I am Neil Van Leeuwen* allows the *I* entity that perceives and does things, whenever the airport is my immediate environment, to use the fact that "Neil Van Leeuwen" in on a ticket and in a database.

We are now ready to answer the important question of how the self-notion is constituted.

5 Question 3: How Can We Characterize the Self-Notion?

We've seen that the self-notion is a first-story notion. Let's consider another example that will allow us to characterize it more precisely.

While on the rowing machine in the gym, I notice that someone doesn't smell too good. At this point, I have two linked notions. I have a first-floor olfactory buffer, which tracks the odor. But I also have a third-floor, objective notion/file of the person who doesn't smell too good. Once I leave, I can use this third-floor notion to think about that person, even after the smell is gone, under the description *the person who didn't smell too good*. But now suppose I'm still in the gym and go to a part of it where there are no other people, and suppose I notice the smell persists. Thinking through the possibilities, I come to the thought:

$$\{\text{Self-Notion}\}\ \text{am}\ [\text{The Person Who Doesn't Smell Too Good}_{\text{OlfactoryBuffer/PersonWhoSmells}}]$$

I learn *I* don't smell too good. I realized this by seeing that *I* was in a part of the gym without other people, while smelling the odor still.

Let's pause on the locution just used: "seeing that *I* was in a part of the gym". I didn't see my*self*. Rather, my visual percepts were of a part of the gym with no one else in it. So why does it feel so natural to use the word "I" in describing what I saw?

The answer is that my visual buffer of nearby surroundings feeds location ideas into my self-notion. This is the crucial point. Part of what it is *to be* a self-notion is to receive location ideas from one's visual or other per-

[17] Let me just stress that this example is purely fictitious. I have no idea whether Barry Sanders has a ferret.

ceptual buffers, including especially the buffers for normally self-informative ways of knowing. More precisely:

> Claim 1: Part of what constitutes the self-notion is that its ideas of the location of the individual it is about *come from* (at least in part) the perceptual buffers of the individual in whose mind the self-notion occurs.

This claim falls under Perry's more general claim about what makes for a self-notion. Recall *Perry's Thesis*: "[S]elf-notions are those that have the special role of being the repository for information gained in normally self-informative ways and the motivator for actions done in normally self-effecting ways" (Perry 2002c: 205). Claim 1 is a corollary of Perry's Thesis, so long as looking around (taking in one's environment through a visual buffer) is counted as a normally self-informative way of learning where one is.[18] We can add:

> Claim 2: Part of what constitutes the self-notion is that its ideas of the bodily state of the individual it is about *come from* (at least in part) the sensations of pleasure and pain in the individual in whose mind the self-notion occurs.
>
> Claim 3: Part of what constitutes the self-notion is that its ideas of the bodily posture of the individual it is about *come from* (at least in part) proprioceptive sensations in the individual in whose mind the self-notion occurs.

We could carry on indefinitely with further corollaries. But the general idea is clear: Part of what makes for a self-notion is its associated file packed with information gained in certain ways; those are not generally ways of information acquisition like reading a book; rather, they include cognitive activities like looking, feeling, and touching—ways of information acquisi-

---

[18] Note the immunity to error through misidentification: you can be wrong about what you see when you look around to learn your location, but you can't be wrong about *whose* location it is you're learning about by looking around. The relevant quotation: "A perceptual state S is a normally self-informative way of knowing that one is φ if the fact that a person is in state S normally carries information that the person in state S is φ and normally does not carry the information that any other person is φ" (Perry 2002c: 204). I do think, to be honest, there is some looseness to what counts as a *normally self-informative way of knowing*. Sometimes Perry seems to characterize this concept in terms of the identity between whom the way of knowing is about and the person who knows in that way. But other times the immunity to error through misidentification is what's important, as is suggested by the quotation in this footnote. The extension of the concept characterized in the latter way is broader than its extension characterized in the former way. But it seems to me that the broader extension is still useful in characterizing the self-notion, which is the main project here, so I focus on that and thus include perceptual states of the external world among the normally self-informative ways of knowing.

tion in which the agent whose situation is learned about is architecturally guaranteed to be the same as the agent learning.

Perry's Thesis includes "normally self-effecting ways of acting". What are those? *Those are ways of acting in which the agent affected by an action normally just is the agent.* Perry gives the example moving one's arm in such a way as to bring a cup to one's lips (Perry 2002c: 205). That's not a way of giving water to someone else; it's a way of giving water to yourself. A host of actions fall in this category: scratching, lifting food to your mouth, holding a flower to your nose, wrapping yourself in a blanket, and so on. These are all quite basic actions, and to perform them, I do *not* conceive myself under a detached, third-personal notion, like [the guy in office 735A with a blue shirt]. Rather, I find that *I* {self-notion} desire water.

Let's flesh this picture out. Desires are mental structures that motivate action. As such, they are typically structures that represent something as happening—often they represent a certain agent as getting something. So, often, a desire is structured as: {agent notion}/[agent notion] gets {object notion}/[object notion].[19] Now we ask again: How can we define *self-notion*? We've already identified a class of actions independently: The normally self-effecting ways of acting. So, along with Perry, we can propose: the self-notion is what occupies the agent notion role in those desires that motivate normally self-effecting ways of action.

This view could yield hundreds of additional corollaries to Perry's Thesis, but I'll just mention three.

> Claim 4: Part of what constitutes the self-notion is that the self-notion occupies the agent notion role in desires that issue in lifting drinking vessels to one's lips.
>
> Claim 5: Part of what constitutes the self-notion is that the self-notion occupies the agent notion role in desires that issue in scratching oneself.
>
> Claim 6: Part of what constitutes the self-notion is that the self-notion occupies the agent notion role in desires that issue in wrapping oneself in a blanket.

These Claims, of course, only apply to agents prone to doing the actions in question and for whom those actions would be normally self-effecting; basically, humans. We could, by way of contrast, imagine aliens who never drink or wrap themselves in blankets, and to have their itches scratched they call the central Martian scratching agency. For such aliens, other claims would be needed to define the self-notion, ones that appeal to the normally

---

[19] The relevant points will go through for other desire structures.

self-effecting actions *for them*. But Claims 4–6 do well for human self-notions.

The picture Claims (1–6) paint is of the self-notion as the informational node linking normally self-informative ways of knowing (and agent-relative knowledge more generally) to normally self-effecting ways of acting. Because these ways of knowing and acting can be defined independently of the self-notion, by way of agent-relative information and the identity relation, this way of defining *self-notion* is clearly not circular.

Let's use this picture to address our example of Jean Valjean. Valjean has more than one notion that refers to himself. Only one of them is the self-notion. Which is it? Why isn't the [24601] notion the self-notion? We now have an answer. Lacking the appropriate cognitive links, [24601] is not the repository of normally self-informative ways of knowing and is not implicated in the motivation of normally self-effecting ways of acting. Before Vajean realizes he's 24601, seeing a fence in font of him doesn't feed into Valjean's 24601 notion. *His* fence percepts don't give him ideas about where 24601 is. Nor does Valjean's (seemingly altruistic) desire that 24601 be well nourished cause Valjean to lift food to his *own* mouth. But now suppose Valjean has another notion that refers to himself; call this notion V. Suppose further that when Valjean sees a fence, the idea of facing a fence is fed into Valjean's V notion. He thinks: {V} is/am [facing a fence]. Furthermore, when Valjean feels a toothache, the idea of having a toothache is put in the V file. And whenever Valjean desires that V have a drink and there is a cup of water nearby, this causes Valjean's arm to lift the cup to his own lips. If V has all these relational properties—in short, if V satisfies Perry's Thesis and the corollary Claims 1–6—then V *just is* Valjean's self-notion.

So far, the self-notion seems primitive, a repository for basic information and motivator for basic actions. But the self-notion *can* link to third-story objective knowledge. The plug sticking up from the self-notion can connect with sockets dangling down from the third floor, sockets that dangle down from notion/files such as [24601] or [the shabby pedagogue on the bus]. In Valjean's case, {V} becomes linked to [24601]. When that happens, if Valjean knew 24601 was going to solitary, he would realize *he* is going to solitary. He comes to anticipate as host of normally self-informative, agent-relative information: seeing darkness, feeling hunger, feeling a damp stone floor. And he may try to hide a bottle of water under his shirt, anticipating he'll need it to perform the self-effecting action of bringing a drinking vessel to his lips. In short, his previously detached knowledge about 24601 becomes suddenly pertinent to how he sees, feels, and acts on the environment immediately around him. The self-notion is not merely the informational node linking agent-relative knowledge to normally self-effecting action; it is also the node that can link such ground-level epistemic and pragmatic ways of knowing and acting to objective knowledge that happens to pertain to the self. As Perry puts it, "My self-notion can be both tied to an epistemic/pragmatic relation and serve as a permanent file for myself" (Perry 2002c: 206).[20]

6 Conclusion: What Perry Accomplishes

What does Perry's theory of self-notions, self-belief, and self-knowledge accomplish? I think the biggest accomplishment is that the theory comes as close as possible to characterizing what it takes for a cognitive system to have self-knowledge, without resorting to descriptions from the inside—or first-personal, phenomenological descriptions. It's true that Perry mentions sensations, like feeling flush, in exemplifying normally self-informative ways of knowing. But the phenomenology of those states is not what's important to Perry's project. Rather, what's important is (1) the logical relation of *identity* between the person those states carry information about and the person who is in those states and (2) the architecture of the cognitive system that ensures that identity.

To summarize, the first theoretical step[21] is independently to classify ways of acquiring information and forms of action. This yields the categories of agent-relative information, normally self-informative ways of knowing, and normally self-effecting ways of acting. Once these forms of information reception and action have been classified, Perry can use them noncircularly to define the self-notion; the self-notion is the repository of information acquired from the normally self-informative ways of knowing and is a constituent in desires that motivate self-effecting ways of acting. Filling these roles, the self-notion is also able to relate the self of the here-and-now, which must drink water and avoid tree stumps, to normally de-

[20] Note that Perry's way of looking at self-knowledge makes salient a logically possible form of amnesia that, as far as I know, never occurs. One could remember all of one's biographical information, but still have forgotten which person, of the persons one has knowledge about, one is. For example, if I had this form of amnesia, I might still remember Neil Van Leeuwen's history, but still not know whether I am he or I am Albert Newen, some of whose history I also know, albeit to a much lesser extent. I think it argues in favor of Perry's view that this form of amnesia never happens. For one thing that must prevent it from happening is that some of my knowledge of Neil Van Leeuwen's history comes in the form of perceptual memories, like visual memories. Saying that such memories are first-personal and saying they encode agent-relative information is almost saying the same thing, which argues in favor of seeing the agent-relative information as self-notion constituting.

[21] In order of logical priority, not necessarily in order of presentation.

tached information, like information about which stream has fresh water and which trees attract poison oak.

The next theoretical moves are clear. The concept of a self-notion can be used to characterize self-belief—beliefs in which the self-notion is a constituent—which can be used to characterize self-knowledge.

Thus, Perry manages to give a theory of self-knowledge that starts with very humble origins. The categories of agent-relative knowledge, normally self-effecting actions, and normally self-informative ways of knowing apply just as well to cats and dogs. Dogs scratch their ears, just as humans do, and cats feel their hair standing on end, just as humans feel their hearts race. But Perry shows that from these humble origins is constructed the core, the self-notion, of what is often regarded as humankind's singular cognitive achievement: self-knowledge.

Acknowledgments

I'd like to thank Wes Holliday, Thad Metz, Albert Newen, and Raphael van Riel for comments on earlier drafts of this paper. Most of all, I'd like to thank John Perry, without whom I *couldn't* have written this!

7

Perry on Personal Identity

RAPHAEL VAN RIEL

1 Introduction

There are a number of philosophically important questions related to the concept of a person and to personal identity. The concept of a person is, as Perry noted (1983b/2002B1: 119), fundamental for our understanding and evaluation of ethical claims; it plays a crucial role in politics and juridical contexts; and, since persons are "our primary examples of knowers and agents" (ibid.), an approach to what persons are should, as Perry claims, figure in any comprehensive epistemology and metaphysics. In these contexts, properties such as the property of being a moral agent, the property of being responsible for the outcome of an action, the property of being human, the property of being rational, etc. are investigated, and all of these properties seem to be intimately related to personhood. Other questions relate to the social identity of persons, the factors which influence the way we and others conceive of ourselves, gender, and the relations between persons and (other) animals. Another question concerns the metaphysics of persons in the following sense: We may want to know under which conditions a person x is identical to a person y. For example, we may want to know under which conditions, or in virtue of which facts it is true to say of the old man that he is the same person as the young lad in the picture taken fifty years ago. This question is interesting in itself—it concerns the question of how persons exist over time, or, more technically, how they *persist*

Identity, Language, and Mind: An Introduction to the Philosophy of John Perry.
Albert Newen and Raphael van Riel (eds.).

as persons.[1] An appropriate answer to this question will bear upon several broader issues: When we want to know why we should care about what happens to us in the future, it might be interesting to know what makes it true to say that in the future, we will be the persons we are now. Similarly, these considerations play a crucial role for juridical issues: Ideally, people are sued, tried in a court, and sentenced *after they* committed a crime. If our juridical practice is justified at all, it will be justified only if the person who actually committed the crime is the same as the person who is sentenced. Although we have criteria at hand to decide when a person at a time t is the same as a person at another time t* (i.e. the observable spatio-temporal continuity of the respective bodies) it is not easy to see *in virtue of which* facts the former is identical to the latter. This becomes obvious once we consider possible (and more or less fictitious) cases of person-fission, mind-transference, or person-fusion. In a fission case (the case we will focus on below), we are faced with a situation in which the mind associated with one single body somehow turns into two minds associated with two bodies. This can be interpreted as a special case of mind-transference, in which one person's mind ends up in a body it was not associated with before. A case of person-fusion is a case in which two minds become associated with one single body. Modern versions of such cases usually refer to specific kinds of operations, such as brain transplants. Referring to such cases, we can test our intuitions concerning the conditions under which the person who is doped before the operation is the same as the person (or the persons) who wakes up after the operation took place. Building on these intuitions, we can try to shape our ideas about what it is for one person x to be the same person as a person y, and to come up with an account of personal identity. Intuitions, though, may differ, and a number of independent assumptions may be put into play in order to decide the issue of personal identity. The accounts of personal identity on offer can be divided into two classes: psychological, or, as Perry labels them, 'mentalist' accounts, and physiological accounts.[2]

1.1 Psychological and Physiological Accounts of Personal Identity

Roughly, physiological accounts assume that relations among non-psychological aspects of a person are sufficient to give an illuminating account of when a person x is identical to a person y (as, for example, de-

---

[1] Note that, as Olson (1997a) points out, knowing when a person x is identical to a person y is not the same as knowing under which conditions a person x is identical to some y, given that persons are not essentially persons. For example, one may want to hold that John Perry once was an embryo and that embryos are not persons.

[2] A third alternative consists in taking the notion of personal identity to be basic.

fended by Ayer (1936), Olson (1997b), van Inwagen (1990), and Williams (1956–57, 1970, 1973)). Psychological accounts deny that. Most prominently, these have been defended in different forms by Grice (1941), Lewis (1976), Parfit (1971), Shoemaker (1963, 1970, 1997, 1999), and, in particular, by Perry (1972, 1975a, 1976a and b, 1978B, 1983b; see also the collection of papers "Identity, Personal Identity, and the Self" (Perry 2002B1)), and they can be traced back to Locke (1694). According to psychological accounts, an illuminating account of when a person x is identical to a person y essentially involves the use of mental concepts—the most prominent being the concept of memory. Perry's account of personal identity is a mentalist account; it builds upon the idea that for a person x (at a time t > t*) to be identical to a person y at t*, there must be some relevant mental relation holding between x at t and y at t*. In order to make the idea of persons at times more transparent, we should make use of the idea of a *person-stage*. If a person x has F at a time t, then there is a person-stage y which exists at t and has F. Person-stage talk does not commit us to the assumption that persons are (units of) person-stages, and it is compatible with the idea that persons consist of a number of person stages. If the latter view is correct, then in a sense, persons are units which persist through time and which consist of person-stages existing at different times. Thus, on a mentalist account which takes persons to be units of person stages, the glue which holds distinct person stages together (i.e. the relevant relation whose instantiation makes them belong to, or constitute, one single person) is a mental relation holding between these stages. According to physiological accounts which make use of the notion of a person stage, the glue which holds together distinct person stages is a physiological relation holding between these stages. Perry takes persons to be units of person stages which have to instantiate a specific mental relation in order to belong to one person.

1.2 Aspects of Perry's Discussion of Personal Identity

Perry developed his account (i) by defending the general mentalist strategy against criticisms (Perry 1976a and b), (ii) by defending and re-interpreting a specific mentalist (namely, the Gricean) strategy (Grice 1941), which explicates the notion of personhood at least partially in terms of memory (cf. Perry 1975b), and (iii) by building upon his interpretation of the logical form of one sort of identity statements (esp. Perry 1972; for reference to other papers of Perry's which are dealing with identity statements, see Section 6). His work on personal identity thus includes, in addition to the development of his own account, careful reconstructions of his predecessors and of some rival approaches. Moreover, Perry (1976b and 1983b) focuses on related topics, such as the relevance of personal identity and its relation to the use of folk-psychology in every-day life. In the present paper, I will mainly focus on a reconstruction of Perry's account of personal identity and on part of the background from which it arose, namely, on aspects of Perry's work on the logical form of a specific kind of identity statement. The latter led to his interpretation of accounts of personal identity *as accounts of the conditions under which two constituents or parts of a person belong to a unity, which is a person* (which is not to be confused with an explication of the identity relation). In order to follow the discussion, however, we require a rough idea of the mentalist's and, more specifically, the memory-theorist's view of personal identity. We will be in a position to give an idea of this strategy once we have an idea of Perry's view of the logical form of the relevant kind of identity-statement, namely, instances of sentence-forms like 'x is the same person as y' and 'x and y are the same person'. As we shall see, there are two rival interpretations of the function of the word 'person' here. Under one interpretation, it modifies the word 'identity', such that 'personal identity' designates or signifies a specific identity-relation. Under another interpretation (favored by Perry), it does not modify the word 'identity'; rather (and intuitively), its role consists in its enabling us to pick out the right sort of entity referred to by the respective instances of 'x' and 'y'.

We shall proceed as follows: In Section 2, the relevant aspects of Perry's work on the logical form of identity-statements will be summarized. In Section 3, some features of the mentalist strategy will be highlighted. In Section 4, a fictional example discussed in Perry 1972 will be introduced. In Section 5, we will be in a position to introduce the account Perry developes in evaluating the example. Finally (Section 6), I shall briefly summarize related aspects of Perry's work on personal identity and suggest further readings on related topics.

2 The Logical Form of (Some) Identity-Statements

For many metaphysicians, it is common to say that to account for the metaphysical status of *Fs* is to account for the criteria of identity of *Fs*. To account for the metaphysics of persons is, then, to account for the identity criteria of persons. Thereby, metaphysical considerations are related to identity-talk. Let us, first, make this connection transparent in order to get, second, an idea of Perry's interpretation of the logical form of the relevant identity statements.

2.1 Some Background: Metaphysics and Identity-Criteria

The idea of identity-criteria is in need of explanation—being an identity-criterion can be understood in at least two different ways, only one of which is important for metaphysical concerns. Consider the following two identity-criteria for mereological wholes (and assume that they are correct; modal operators are suppressed). A mereological whole is, by definition, nothing over and above its parts:

1. x is identical to y iff for any z, z is a part of x iff z is a part of y.
2. We may come to know that x is identical to y by observing a spatio-temporal continuity between x and y.

The former is (if correct) interesting in a metaphysical sense. It gives us the metaphysically relevant identity-criteria for mereological wholes. It is one way of more carefully expressing the idea that a mereological whole is fully individuated by its parts. The latter is interesting in an epistemological respect. It gives us criteria under which we are justified in identifying a mereological sum x with a mereological sum y. Here, we are interested in criteria of the former kind—to account for the metaphysics of personhood is to give a criterion of the first kind. The second can be labeled a 'criterion for identification'. In contrast, in metaphysics we are concerned with criteria of identity. But would any criterion do which does not appeal to *us coming to know about* the identity of an object x with an object y? Compare 1. with 3. (and assume that 3. is correct):

3. x is identical to y iff, if x were to fall on my foot, then x's falling on my foot would be y's falling on my foot.

Even if 3. is true, it is not very interesting if we want to account for the identity criteria of objects of a kind to which x belongs. Can we give at least an intuitive idea of the difference between 1. and 3.? The idea behind 1. can be described as follows: For something to be a mereological whole just is for it to be individuated by its parts; if x is a mereological whole and y is a mereological whole, and if x = y, then x = y *because* x and y have exactly the same parts. However, it is not the case that if x is a mereological whole and y is a mereological whole, and x = y, then x = y *because* it is true that if x were to fall on my foot, then x's falling on my foot would be y's falling on my foot. This gives a rough idea of the kind of identity criteria we are interested in in the metaphysics of persons: We want to arrive at criteria which give an insight into the nature of the objects whose metaphysics we are accounting for; we want to know in virtue of which facts it is true to say that some x is the same F as some y (if this is true).

The relation between issues concerning identity statements and issues concerning personal identity should by now be obvious: In order to account for personal identity, we have to develop an appropriate candidate for interesting truth-conditions of sentences of the form 'x and y are the same person' (and of sentences of similar sentence-forms). However, this still leaves room for two rival interpretations of how such truth-conditions are to be shaped.

2.2 Two Accounts of the Logical Form of Identity-Statements

These two interpretations depend upon different interpretations of the functioning of the term 'person' in such sentences (or, more generally, of the functioning of instances of 'F' in sentences of the form 'x is the same F as y', or 'the Fs x and y are identical', and the like). One can get an intuitive idea of the difference between these two interpretations by first introducing the relevant consequences these rival accounts have. According to one interpretation, the difference between persons and mereological wholes is to be cashed out in terms of different identity relations. If a given x is the same mereological whole as a given y, this means for the mereological whole x to stand in a *specific* relation of identity to y, namely, the mereological whole relation of identity. Put differently: If mereological wholes differs in their identity-criteria from persons, then, on that account, if Marie Henri Beyle is identical to Stendhal, and a given mereological whole x is identical to a given y, then the two occurrences of '_is identical to _' will pick out different relations. Perry denies that. According to Perry's view, the difference between "personal identity" and "mereological whole identity" is not to be cashed out in terms of different identity-relations, but rather in terms of differences between the objects picked out by the expressions referring to persons and the expressions referring to mereological wholes in the relevant identity statements (or, in general, the entities which form the kind identified by the relevant general term 'F' in an identity statement of the relevant sort). Let us try to give a more thorough interpretation of this difference first and then turn to an argument in favor of Perry's interpretation.

Under the interpretation Perry opposes, an account of personal identity is an account of a specific kind of identity-relation, namely, the personal-identity relation. Let us label this account the *Multiple Identity Relations Account* (MIR). Under a rival interpretation—the interpretation Perry favors—it is an account of the metaphysics of persons, building on the concept of personhood. Let us label this account the *Singular Identity Relation*

Account (SIR).[3] In order to get a more thorough idea of MIR's and SIR's interpretations of the functioning of 'person' in the relevant identity-statements, we should step back for a moment and reflect upon the role terms of this kind play in identity statements in general. That is: How does 'F' affect the truth-conditions in sentences of the form 'x and y are the same F'? An answer to this question will reflect the intuitive distinction between giving an account of a specific relation of personal identity on the one hand and giving an account of personhood on the other, in terms of the logical form of sentences which state the relevant identities.

According to MIR, 'F' is interpreted as a modifier that works on 'same'. According to this interpretation, for x and y to be the same F is to be the same in a very specific sense, namely, in the F-sense of '_is the same as _'. For x and y to be the same person is, thus, for them to be person-identical. For them to be the same physical object is, thus, for them to be physical-object identical. According to this view, some x and some y may very well be F-identical without being G-identical, if F and G are distinct. Accordingly, x and y may (at least in principle) be person-identical without being physical-object identical.

According to SIR, 'F' is interpreted as a sortal whose function consists in its contribution to reference-fixing: Intuitively, it ensures that we pick out the right entity by the sentence's singular terms. Accordingly, for x and y to be the same person is for x to be a person and for y to be a person, and to be the same. According to this (Fregean) interpretation, we do not get different kinds of identity—there just is identity. Thus, according to this view, if x and y are the same physical object and if x and y are the same person, then x and y are the same, and they are persons, and they are physical objects. Let us illustrate this distinction by reflecting upon three examples, one of which is analogous to the MIR-interpretation of identity statements and two of which are analogous to the SIR interpretation of identity statements.

Assume that Peter and Mary are *relatives*. The question may very well arise whether or not they are *relatives by blood*, or *relatives by marriage*. These relations are distinct—standing in the relative by blood relation to somebody is different from standing in the relative by marriage relation to him or her. Now, in the sentence 'Peter and Mary are relatives by marriage', 'by marriage' modifies the meaning of 'relative'. It determines the relevant relation of *being a relative of*. Similarly, according to MIR, in the sentence 'Stendhal and Marie Henri Beyle are the same person', 'person' determines

[3] Note that these labels are not taken from Perry's work. The distinction is (abstracting away from a number of details) here drawn in a way which makes it suitable for the present discussion. Originally, Perry (1970a and 1978b) discussed this topic criticizing Geach's interpretation of 'the same F' (Geach 1962, 1967 and 1972).

which sort of sameness-(or identity-)relation is alluded to in the sentence. On this view, Marie Henri Beyle and Stendhal may be person-identical without being physical object-identical, just as Peter and Mary may be relatives by marriage without being relatives by blood.

To get an idea of Perry's rival interpretation, SIR, let us now consider the following case: "The United Kingdom and the US are closely related states." Here, we do not use the term 'states' in order to determine a relation of being state-closely-related. We introduce it to say that the states, referred to by 'UK' and 'US', are closely related. Both are states, and they are closely related. We introduce the term 'state' to disambiguate 'United Kingdom' and 'US', which can be used to refer to a state (a political entity), a territory, and, maybe (under some old-fashioned interpretation) a culture. Similarly, Perry takes the term 'person' in the predicate '_are the same person' to help us individuate the object picked out by the instances of 'x' and 'y'. Here is another example: "Creationism and Darwinism are incompatible views." Here, it follows that Creationism is a view, that Darwinism is a view, and that these views are incompatible. Assuming that Creationism and Darwinism are incompatible views, we do not commit ourselves to the assumption that Darwinism and Creationism are view-incompatible (i.e. instantiate a specific incompatibility-relation specified by the term 'view'). So, the difference between SIR and MIR results from a difference in the analysis of the functioning of (relevant) general terms in identity statements. But how do we decide between these two interpretations?

For one thing, one might assume that the burden of proof rests with MIR—it is this view which is less economical, and it is this view which conflicts with the *prima facie* plausible assumption that we should not postulate ambiguities without positive reason. Moreover, there is positive reason in favor of Perry's interpretation. The following fictional situation, described by Perry (1972), gives reason to conclude that SIR is correct—it shows that it seems natural to assume that the functioning of 'F' in statements of the form 'x is the same F as y' consists in its contribution to the identification of the referents of the singular terms involved in this sentence, rather than to specify a specific identity-relation.

Alf has difficulties in judging whether or not a table he sees at one time is the table he sees at another time, and that this is so for some principled reasons. That is: Alf does not know under which conditions the table he sees at one time would be the table he sees at another time. Assume that Alf fully understands the claim that 2 + 2 = 4 and the claim that Marie Henri Beyle is identical to Stendhal (or that Marie Henri Beyle is the same person as Stendhal). Now, assume that for a table x to be identical to a table y is for x to stand in a specific identity-relation to y (as MIR would have it). On this assuption, Alf is *lacking the relevant concept of table-identity*.

But following SIR, one might want to suggest that Alf (as described above) knows what it is for a table x to be *the same* table as y—it is for x to be identical to y, in the same sense in which the mereological whole constituted by John Perry and this volume is identical to the mereological whole constituted by the philosopher this volume is about and the volume you are just reading, in which 2 is identical to 1 + 1, and in which Marie Henri Beyle is identical to Stendhal. What Alf is lacking, then, is an appropriate concept of a table (or of an artifact)—he does not know what these things are. Now, *prima facie* this latter solution seems plausible: Alf has the concept of identity without having the concept of a table or of an artifact. Here is why: Alf understands the question of when a thing x observed at one time is identical to a thing y observed at another time. Accordingly, Alf is in a position to know that for the answer to this question to be 'yes', the thing x has to be identical to the thing y. But then, his lack of an idea of when table x is identical to table y has nothing to do with lacking the concept of the relevant identity relation. Rather, he does not know what we are talking about using expressions such as 'this table' (accompanied by an appropriate gesture). This lack of understanding points to the fact that he does not know what tables are, and that, therefore, the functioning of 'table' in 'this table is the same as this table' consists in its contribution to the identification of the object we are talking about. This seems to generalize, such that the contribution of 'person' in sentences of the form 'x is the same person as y' just is its contribution to the identification of the object we are talking about using sentences of this form—just as SIR would have it.

In summary: If 2 is identical to 1 + 1 and if Marie Henri Beyle is identical to Stendhal, then there is one R such that R(2, 1 + 1) and R(Marie Henri Beyle, Stendhal). The difference between an identity criterion for numbers and an identity criterion for persons does not stem from the fact that number-identity is different from person-identity, but rather from the fact that whether or not a person x is identical to a person y depends upon facts of a different kind from facts upon which number identities depend. To say that there is a difference between number identity and personal identity is to say that persons and numbers are different things. Most importantly, the metaphysical question of what makes a person x identical to a person y depends on the nature of persons, rather on the nature of a specific kind of being identical.

But what is the relation we characterize when we give an account of personal identity? According to SIR, it is not a specific identity relation. Recall the idea of person-stages. Perry holds that personhood consists in a specific unity relation—a relation in virtue of which the thing writing this paper now and the thing which was working on this paper yesterday belong to the same unity, namely, me. Unity relations for bodies may differ from unity relations for persons. Thus, unity relations are not to be conflated with identity relations. An account of personal identity will, given this picture, then be an account of a relation *R* in virtue of which distinct person stages belong to the same person (i.e. a unity of person stages).

3 The Mentalist Strategy

We are now in a position to characterize Perry's version of the mentalist strategy, which builds on the idea of a unity relation: According to Perry (and others) the unity relation is (at least partly) a mental relation. The mentalist strategy can roughly be outlined as follows: For the thing which writes this essay now and the thing which was working on this essay yesterday to belong to the same unity, or to the same person, there must be some mental relation between these two things. According to one strategy, which Perry attributes mainly to Locke (1694) and Grice (1941), this relation is a relation which has to be cashed out in terms of *memory*—the thing that worked on this essay yesterday and the thing which works on this essay now belong to the same person only if (and if so, at least partly in virtue of the fact that) the thing working on this paper now can remember (or could be in a position to remember, under favorable circumstances) what happened to the thing that was working on this essay yesterday. Let us assume that the overall strategy is correct, or at least *prima facie* plausible, as long as it can be defended against various criticisms. In order to mark an important distinction between memory accounts and Perry's account, and to present Perry's important counter-argument against memory-accounts, we should briefly reflect upon Perry's discussion of the threat of the alleged circularity of the Gricean theory of personal identity (Perry 1975b).

3.1 Perry's Defense and Re-Interpretation of the Gricean View

Perry defended Grice's view against the threat of circularity, which, as he puts it, could be raised by those who believe the concept of personal identity to be primitive (e.g. Butler 1736 and Reid 1785: Essay III, Chapter 5 and 6). Roughly, Grice characterizes a person as a set of states which fully consist of experiences at a time. Moreover, being a person is, according to Grice, nothing over and above being this set—it is a *logical construction* fully based on the notions of experience and relations among different experiential states. The glue which holds together the different experiential stages, i.e. the relation which makes a given stage belong to one person rather than another, is, intuitively, a memory-relation. Under favorable circumstances, for the thing which is working on this paper now to belong to the same person as the thing which was working on this paper yesterday, the thing which is working on this paper now (a person stage fully determined by its present experiences) has, or could have had, recollections of what happened to the thing which was working on this paper yesterday, which is, again, a person stage consisting of the experiences present at the time of its existence. Now, one might assume that to give an idea of when this is the case, we have to use the notion of a person in order to describe the conditions under which we *actually* remember, or could have remembered, what happened to a person stage existing prior to the time the remembering occurs (or could have occurred). To fully spell out this idea, and to give an appropriate characterization of Perry's response would take us too far. We should just assume that, at least at first glance, *whose* experiences we *actually* remember (or could have remembered) depends upon the fact that these experiences actually were *our* experiences and that, therefore, we cannot give a non-circular account of personal identity (the unity-relation R) in terms of memory relations among person-stages.

Perry argues that this is not the case: We can refer to a (hypothesized) underlying causal process which leads from one experience to another without invoking the notion of a person. As Perry noted, by articulating the memory-view in terms of a causal process which connects different experiences, he deviates from the Gricean idea: According to Perry, the concept of a person cannot be fully accounted for in terms of experiences and memory relations (for a detailed sketch of this and other differences, see Perry 1975b: Section 5). Rather, we use memory relations in order to refer to the relevant causal process, which gives us the relevant unity relation for person-stages. Thus, Perry's version of the mentalist account should not be regarded as being a classical memory-theorist account. In a nutshell, Perry's version of the mentalist account consists in the idea that the unity relation is a causal process relation *underlying* different memory and other mental relations. Person-stages thus belong to one unity (one person) if and only if these person stages instantiate this process relation. This gives a sufficient idea of the unity relation. It does not, however, give us an idea yet of how this criterion of identity connects to sentences of the form 'x is the same person as y'. Perry's view of this connection is the target of the next section. The unity-relation will be referred to as '*R*'. Before turning to a more detailed version of Perry's solution, we should briefly reflect upon the path via which Perry arrives at his conclusions.

Recall what Perry had to say about the logical form of identity-statements: The role of expressions such as 'person' in statements of the form 'x is the same person as y' consists in their contribution to the identification of the referent of the relevant sentences' singular terms. This is a *semantic* characterization. A more detailed account of the semantics of talk about persons will give an idea of how the relevant identity-statements are connected to the unity-relation *R*. Perry pursues this goal in the following way: He discusses an example which leads to three seemingly inconsistent statements to which the mentalist seems committed. Perry shows that there is an interpretation of the mentalist approach to personal identity according to which appropriate renderings of said statements are not incompatible. The interpretation takes the form of an interpretation of the relevant part or fragment of English which is supposed to make its metaphysical underpinnings transparent. Three candidates for expressing such an interpretation are discussed, the *branch-language*, the *person-stage language*, and the *lifetime-language*. The *branch-language* and the *person-stage* language are rejected. The discussion of these languages leads to two important desiderata that an account of personal identity should meet. The lifetime-language does meet these desiderata. So, let us first introduce the example and then turn to Perry's discussion (Perry 1972).

4 A Problem for the Mentalist?

Three persons, Brown, Jones, and Smith, enter a hospital to get brain rejuvenations. Roughly, in brain rejuvenation the mental structure of your brain (a brain's mental structure is what determines your mental life, including memories) is conserved, but the gray matter is replaced. During surgery, the brains of Brown and Smith are destroyed (say, by accident) before anyone was able to copy these brains' mental structures. Jones' mental structure is then copied three times, and the three brains are put into Jones', Brown's and Smith's heads. To make things even more complicated, Jones dies a little later. Let us call the person which has Brown's body and Jones' memories 'Brown-Jones' and the person which has Smith's body and Jones' memories 'Smith-Jones'. Both, Brown-Jones and Smith-Jones, claim to be Jones (although they are somewhat irritated by the bodies they see instead of the body they expect to see when taking a look at themselves).

It follows that Brown-Jones and Smith-Jones have the same memories, namely, those of Jones. Let us grant that if the idea of there being a relevant mental relation which makes for personal identity (i.e. the unity relation) is sound, then it is instantiated by person stages of Jones and Brown-Jones, as well as by person-stages of Jones and Smith Jones. The mentalist seems thus committed to the following two claims:

(i) Brown-Jones is Jones.

(ii) Smith-Jones is Jones.

Why is she committed to these claims? Because she is committed to the idea that the two persons who are now Smith-Jones and Brown-Jones bear the relevant mental relation to the person stages which existed before the operation took place. Thus, in a sense, before the operation took place, Brown-Jones was Jones, and before the operation took place, Smith-Jones was Jones. However, we should not assume that Brown-Jones is identical to Smith-Jones—they share some properties, but not all properties. They are different persons. Thus, the mentalist seems, in addition, to be committed to the following claim:

(iii) It is not the case that Smith-Jones is Brown-Jones.

But this seems to imply a straightforward contradiction: If Brown-Jones is Jones and Smith Jones is Jones, it is impossible that Brown-Jones is not Smith-Jones. Thus, (i)-(iii) seem to be incompatible. However, as Perry argues, the intuitions underlying (i)-(iii) can be saved. As already mentioned, Perry introduces three rival reconstructions of this fragment of English: the branch-language, the person-stage language, and the lifetime-language. Perry's discussion of these "languages" involves a number of subtleties we cannot discuss here. The branch-language and the person-stage language will be introduced fully in terms of the ontological commitments they involve. Their discussion mainly serves a dialectical purpose—each of the two languages is deficient in (at least) one respect. These aspects are identified in order to develop a language which is in a better shape—the lifetime-language.

5 Perry's Theory of Personal Identity

5.1 The Branch-Language

If sentences (i)-(iii) were to be reconstructed in the branch-language, then in asserting these sentences, one would be committed to the following:

Persons are branches. Branches are sets of exactly those person-stages which bear the relevant unity-relation *R* to each other. Loosely speaking (and using our fictional example): The person-stages which coincided with the existence of Smith-Jones and the person-stages which coincided with the existence of Jones form one person, and the person stages of Brown-Jones and the person stages which coincided with the existence of Jones form another person. More precisely: A set of person-stages is a branch iff all the members of the set have (the relevant unity-relation) *R* to each other and no stage which has *R* to all members of the set is not a member.

This suggests that before the operation took place, there was no single person named 'Jones'—rather, there were two persons, Smith-Jones and Brown-Jones which shared a common part for some time. Unfortunately, we were unable to identify either Smith-Jones or Brown-Jones before the operation took place. The term 'Jones' did not, despite appearance, actually refer. This, however, seems to be an undesirable consequence. Talking to Jones before the operation took place, we were actually talking to one person, and talking about Jones using the name 'Jones', we were able to refer to a person. These intuitions should, if possible, turn out true on any appropriate account of personal identity. Thus, an appropriate account of personal-identity should meet *desideratum one*: Before the operation took place, the name 'Jones' did actually refer to a person. But can we, then, save the truth of statements (ii) and (iii)? Recall the motivation for assuming that the mentalist is committed to these claims. Mentalists should believe in (ii) and (iii) because the mentalist is committed to the idea that the two persons who are now Smith-Jones and Brown-Jones bear the relevant mental relation to the person stages which existed before the operation took place. However, should we really believe that (ii) and (iii) are implied by (iv) and (v), which express the *relevant* mentalist assumption:

(iv) Before the operation, Smith-Jones was Jones.
(v) Before the operation, Brown-Jones was Jones?

These sentences seem to express the relevant aspect of the mentalist commitment. Perry suggests that under one interpretation of the functioning of 'before the operation' (and similar expressions in similar sentences), this temporal expression restricts the reference of the names which occur within its scope—intuitively, on this interpretation, it signals *when* the names which occur within its scope must refer for the sentence to turn out true. Stating (iv) and (v) in this sense, we commit ourselves to the assumption that the two persons who are now distinct both were, before the operation, Jones. On this interpretation, we are not committed to the claim that now, after the operation, Brown-Jones is identical to Jones and that now, after the operation, Smith-Jones is identical to Jones. But is it reasonable to assume that actually, English behaves sufficiently similar to a language involving this kind of reference shift? And what are the ontological and semantic commitments which go together with this interpretation? The development of the person-stage language and the lifetime language show how more detailed accounts of this language might look like. A characterization of these languages will enable us to judge the plausibility of the assumption that English is sufficiently similar to a language which behaves in that way.

5.2 The Person-Stage Language

If sentences (iii), (iv), and (v) were to be reconstructed in the person-stage language, one would be committed to the following assumptions: Names do not refer to persons (if they refer at all), as the branch-language would have it, but rather to person-stages themselves. Temporal expressions, working on names, enable us to pick out different person stages at different times. Thus, expressions referring to persons (without temporal qualification) are systematically ambiguous. Using "John Perry" when starting to plan this paper, I probably referred to the person-stage which existed at that time, whereas, when I use "John Perry" now, August 5, 2011, I refer to a person stage which exists at that time, and which is not identical to the former, but rather bears the relevant personal-identity relation to the former. On that account, the referents of our names are not persisting persons, but merely person-stages, which, in fact, may form unities we usually do not refer to when talking about persons using names, indexicals, or descriptions.

But what does this mean for the functioning of 'person' in sentences of the following form: 'This person will be F at t'? It means that the term 'person' does not function as enabling us to pick out the relevant entity, namely, a persisting person, a stage of which can be pointed at, but rather that it behaves like an adverb: It gives the specific way in which the person stage referred to by 'this' will have F at t, namely, via standing in a specific personal-identity relation to some stage which is F at t. It is not the object we refer to at one point in time which will be what we ascribe using the term 'F'; rather, it is another object which bears some relevant relation to the object we refer to at a given time. In saying that I will (hopefully) one day finish this paper, I am not literally saying that I will finish this paper one day, but rather that there is an object which will bear an interesting relation to the referent of 'I' (as used by me now) which will, one day, finish this paper (hopefully). Thus, the intuition that it is literally us who will do what we will do (or who did what we did), turns out to be fundamentally mistaken.

Perry thinks that this is an unnecessary complication we should get rid of if we can—just as we should get rid of the idea that, in general, to be the same F as x is to stand in the F-identity relation to x. Thus, we arrive at two desiderata: An appropriate account of personal identity, first, should capture the intuition that the term 'Jones' actually refers to one person before the operation takes place (from the discussion of the branch-language), and, second, that what happens to Smith-Jones and Brown-Jones was about to happen, in a sense, to the person who existed before the operation took place. The lifetime-language is supposed to meet these two requirements.

5.3 The Lifetime Language

The basic idea is that there are not only Smith-Jones and Brown-Jones (which share their Jones-part), as the branch-language would have it. Rather, there are Smith-Jones and Brown-Jones (sharing their Jones-part), as the branch-language would have it, and there is, in addition, what is intuitively describable as a Y-shaped entity which consists of Smith-Jones *and* Brown-Jones (*including* Jones—their shared part). It is an entity of this latter structure we were able to refer to using the term 'Jones' before the operation took place. Moreover, everything that will happen to Smith-Jones and Brown-Jones after the operation was (literally) about to happen to the referent of 'Jones' as used before the operation took place (the Y-shaped structure); thus, the two conditions are met. The three objects, called 'lifetimes', we thus get are individuated as follows: A set of person-stages is a *lifetime* iff there is one member in this set which is such that all other members bear *R* to it, and every person stage that bears R to it is in the set.

But how exactly does reference function within the lifetime-language? Person-stages can be constituents of a number of lifetimes, but any person-stage will bear a privileged relation to some lifetimes of which it is a member—namely, those lifetimes that consist of all those person-stages which bear *R* to *it*. This privileged relation can be used to spell out the idea of reference shift of names at times, and, thereby, of change in truth-conditions of sentences about persons uttered at different times. Intuitively: 'Before the operation, Smith-Jones is Jones' is true iff before the operation, the entity picked out by the names 'Smith-Jones' is the entity picked out by 'Jones' at that time (and, similarly, for 'Brown-Jones is Jones'). 'Smith-Jones is not Brown-Jones' is true after the operation iff the entity picked out by 'Brown-Jones' after the operation is distinct from the entity picked out by 'Smith-Jones' after the operation. What we initially thought to be primarily about different temporal stages of one object, namely, Jones being Jones at one time, and being Brown-Jones and Smith-Jones at another, is now cast as a claim about the different semantic properties of 'Jones' (and other names), which may vary over time. But how does this strategy work in detail?

The lifetime we can pick out pointing at a person-stage is the lifetime constituted by all those person-stages which bear *R* to it. The main point is that we are not always able to use any person-stage without temporal qualification to refer to any lifetime of which this stage is a member. Before the operation took place, there are just person-stages that give, intuitively speaking, access to the Y-shaped structure. Before the operation, there are no person-stages that are such that all and only the stages of one of the branches bear *R* to it. After the operation takes place, things change: Now, there are no person stages present which are such that all person-stages belonging to the Y-shaped structure bear *R* to it.

Perry introduces a number of technical terms to make this idea more precise: Each person-stage *determines* a lifetime—i.e. the unity which includes all those person-stages which bear *R* to it. Moreover, lifetimes are *determinable* at times: A lifetime *y* is determinable at a time t iff there exists a person-stage at t which determines *y*. Thus, before the operation, neither of the branches is determinable, and after the operation, the Y-shaped structure cannot be determined. Finally, let us introduce the idea of a lifetime *y* being *identified* at a time t by a person-stage s (this is the notion that will be used to specify the relevant reference relation of names at times). A lifetime *y* is identified at t by s iff *y* contains s and y is determinable at t. Thus, sometimes, a lifetime will not be identified by a stage s at a time, despite the fact that it exists and contains s. For example, after the operation took place, the Y-shaped structure is not identified by any of its stages—after the operation, there is no person-stage which determines this lifetime.

Corresponding to the notions of *being determined by a person-stage* and *being identified by a person-stage at a time*, we get two different notions of reference: a name's primary referent and a name's secondary referent(s). Assume that, in the lifetime language, names are directly *assigned* to person-stages. We can assign the name 'Jones' to a person-stage of Jones. A name's *primary referent* is the lifetime determined by the person-stage it is assigned to (here, no temporal qualification is involved). In the case of a pre-operative person-stage of Jones, it will be the Y-shaped lifetime, which, loosely speaking, includes Jones, Smith-Jones and Brown-Jones. A name's *secondary referent at a time t* is the lifetime identified by the person-stage at t to which it is assigned. Thus, sometimes, a name may lack a secondary referent. This will be the case when, at a given time, there is no person-stage that determines the lifetime determined by the person-stage the name is assigned to. In this case, the name is improper at that time. To avoid misunderstandings it is worth noting that, nevertheless, after the operation, we are still able to refer to the Y-shaped lifetime—thus, it is not the case that if a lifetime cannot be determined at a time, we cannot refer to that lifetime at that time. Similarly, it is not the case that if a name, used at t, is assigned to a person-stage which determines a lifetime y but which does not identify y at t, then we cannot refer to y.

Perry suggests that by introducing temporal expressions working on the relevant name, we can get an idea of how a sentence may turn out true even if it involves a name that does not, taken in isolation, have a secondary referent at the time of utterance. What is required is that, at the time fixed by the temporal expression, the name has a secondary referent. Now, temporal expressions may, according to Perry, serve two distinct purposes. Restricting the use of ordinary English, we can introduce the following convention for sentences with which we ascribe properties to persons at times: Temporal expressions precede the name in a sentence iff they fix the time at which the person stage the name is assigned to must identify a lifetime for the sentence to be true. Temporal expressions form part of the predicate in a sentence iff they fix the time at which some person-stage belonging to the relevant lifetime (the secondary referent of the name (at the relevant time)) must exist and must have the property ascribed by the predicate in that sentence, for the sentence to be true. Here is an example.

Assume that after the operation, Smith-Jones was put into room 102 and Brown-Jones was put into room 104. Assume that the name 'Brown-Jones' is assigned to some person-stage which determines the Brown-Jones branch. Then the sentence: 'After the operation, Brown-Jones will be in room 102' is true, even when uttered before the operation. This is so because the secondary referent of 'Brown-Jones' after the operation is the relevant branch which has a person-stage (after the operation) which was put into room 102. For similar reasons, the following sentence is true: 'After the operation, it is not the case that Brown-Jones will be in room 104'. This is so because the secondary referent of 'Brown-Jones' after the operation does not contain a person-stage which is in room 104 after the operation.

Now, assume that 'Jones' is assigned to a stage which determines the Y-shaped structure. Then, the following sentence will turn out true: 'Before the operation, Jones will be in room 102 after the operation, and before the operation, Jones will be in room 104 after the operation'. This sentence is true because the secondary referent of 'Jones' before the operation (i.e. the lifetime identified before the operation by the person-stage to which 'Jones' is assigned) contains a person-stage that will be in room 102 after the operation, and because it contains another person-stage that will be in room 104 after the operation.

On this account, (iii), (iv), and (v) turn out to be compatible: (iii) is no problem at all, when uttered after the operation or when appropriately qualified by a temporal expression. (iv) is true because the secondary referent of 'Smith-Jones' before the operation is the secondary referent of 'Jones'. The secondary referent of 'Brown-Jones' is the secondary referent of 'Jones', so (v) turns out true as well. We thereby come to see that what will happen after the operation was literally about to happen to the secondary referent of 'Jones' before the operation, and, moreover, we come to see that there is one single person we speak to or about when speaking to or about Jones before the operation. Thus, the two desiderata identified above are met.

Let us finish these considerations by briefly returning to Perry's methodological remarks. He puts his thesis about personal identity as follows: The relevant fragment of English just is the lifetime-language—a semantically described piece of language, characterized in terms of referents of names, the functioning of sortals, and the functioning of temporal expressions. The most important move in the lifetime language is to acknowledge that at different times, one and the same name can be used to pick out different, though intimately related lifetimes, and sometimes, names may fail to refer to a lifetime despite the fact that they are assigned to a person-stage which determines a lifetime. The fact that names refer to persons at times is made transparent (in the lifetime-language) by moving the temporal modifier to the beginning of the sentence, when appropriate. One should bear in mind that English is much more flexible, and that sentences of the form 'at t, x is F' do not force us to interpret 'at t' as specifying the time of reference. Perry is pretty clear about this fact, saying that his way of putting things involves a "pardonable regimentation" (Perry 1972/2002B1: 47) of English. Thus, the thesis that the relevant fragment of English is the (or a) lifetime language should be interpreted as follows: The metaphysical underpinnings of the relevant fragment of English can be made transparent by reconstructing it as a lifetime language. Later, however, Perry (1983b: Section 3) suggested a more cautious interpretation of the relation between the relevant fragment of English and the lifetime language. On this occasion, he states that maybe we should not conceive of our concept of a person as fully determining the issue at hand; rather, thought experiments like the one guiding the discussion show that our present concepts underdetermine that matter. The conceptual apparatus underlying the lifetime language then turns out to be constructive in a specific sense: It is one way (amongst others) of responding to a "crisis" (Perry 1983b/2002B1: 132) which is due to considering cases of person-fission or -fusion. Moreover, Perry acknowledges that his view that the question of personal identity is to be based on a thorough distinction between the identity-relation and unity-relations was, maybe, mistaken. However, as he puts it, "[i]t's a very helpful first step" (1983b/2002B1: 133).

6 Related Topics

Perry's work on personal identity is not restricted to the topics discussed in the previous sections. Here, I shall give an overview on related topics Perry discusses. In Perry 1976b, he considers the question of the rationale for being interested, in a special way, in what will happen to us—a topic picked up again in Perry 1983b.

In Perry 1976a, Perry deals with counterarguments against mentalist theories of personal identity, such as those of Bernard Williams (1973). In Perry 1983b we find an interpretation of a number of contributions to the discussion of personal identity, especially those made by Locke, Butler, Shoemaker, Williams, Grice, and Parfit (see above, Section 1). This easily accessible essay sheds light on most of the aspects of Perry's work on personal identity. Similarly, Perry's "Dialogue on Personality and Immortality" (1978B) contains a number of themes pertinent in the debate. Here these themes are presented in a fictional dialogue between Gretchen Weirob, a philosophy teacher, and two friends of hers, Sam Miller, a chaplain, and Dave Cohen, one of her former students. In this brilliant dialogue, the most important positions and lines of argumentation are summarized, and they are presented in a way that comes astonishingly close to what an actual discussion of this topic might look like.

Perry's (2002a), one of the essays on personal identity specially written for the collection of essays "Identity, Personal Identity, and the Self" (Perry 2002B1), contains an account of how our "theory" of the causal processes responsible for the individuation of persons (i.e. those which make for the unity-relation) can be conceived of as a promising candidate for an explication of the unity-relation *R*. For detailed discussions of identity, which shaped his views on personal identity, see Perry 1970a and 1978b. And, finally, Perry's edition 1975E assembles the most relevant classical texts (those of Butler, Locke, and Reid mentioned above as well as Hume (1741)) as well as a number of more recent papers on personal identity (Grice, Nagel, Parfit, Perry, Quinton, Shoemaker, Williams). The Introduction to this book (Perry 1975a) contains a careful exposition of what the problem of personal identity actually is.

8

In Defense of Antecedent Physicalism

DANIEL COHNITZ

1 Introduction

Leo Peters[1] is professor of philosophy, specializing in contemporary American philosophy. One morning, on his way to the department, Leo is hit by a runaway trolley.[2] Fortunately, Leo survives this with just a few scratches, but since the trolley hit his head in the accident, Leo also suffers from a strong headache and a rare case of "Hollywood amnesia"[3]—he forgets that he is Leo Peters[4] and many crucial details about his life, but other than that remembers almost everything else. Despite his strange condition, Leo finds his way to his office.[5]

[1] All characters and events in this story, even those based on real people, are entirely fictional.

[2] There is a complex story to be told about how the trolley ended up there instead of going down an alternative track where it would have run into a group of five promising graduate students. That story involves Gustav Lauben, another colleague from the same department, who made the decision to send the trolley down that track from further up the hill. But this story belongs to another paper.

[3] Hollywood amnesia is the kind of amnesia found in Hollywood movies, typically induced by a bump on the head. It involves "forgetting all or part of your past with no impairment of your ability to deal with the here and now" (Adams 2004).

[4] Except for those details about his identity that he needs to remember for this story to be coherent.

[5] 'What nerd would go to his office after such an accident?' you ask? Don't forget that Leo is a philosopher. They do the funniest things.

Identity, Language, and Mind: An Introduction to the Philosophy of John Perry.
Albert Newen and Raphael van Riel (eds.).

In his office Leo discovers a huge box of personal documents, tapes, and papers with the label 'Leo Peters'[6] on it, and another, even bigger box with the label 'John Perry'. Since Leo remembers that he is a philosophy scholar, and supposed to work on some other philosopher's writings, he infers that before his accident he was working on the writings of at least one of these two guys. Since Leo got his training in continental Europe, Leo believes that the best way to do philosophy is to dig deeply into the mind of one philosophical author by studying every single thing that author has written, and every single detail about that philosopher's life. Leo can't remember who it was he was working on, so he flips a coin to chose one of the boxes, sits down, opens the box with the 'Leo Peters'-label, and starts reading.

Leo is so fascinated by the congenial way of thinking and arguing he finds in Peters' work, that he can't stop reading the contents of the box until he is done, a few days later. Since the box included, in addition to the philosophical writings of Leo Peters, also his minute diaries, old and recent photographs, videotapes, and other personal notes, Leo reconstructs a very comprehensive picture of the guy. Leo learns everything there is to know about Leo Peters, except one thing: that *he* is Leo Peters. Part of the reason why Leo doesn't recognize this is that, although Leo learned from the box how Leo Peters looks, he has forgotten what *he* looks like.

After he is done studying, Leo gets up to go to the next diner to get something to eat and to reflect on how to organize this all encompassing monograph on the philosophy of Leo Peters that he is now ready to write. Opposite of Leo's office door hangs a huge mirror, and when Leo steps out of his office and by the force of habit looks into the mirror, he notices a familiar face. He recognizes that he looks exactly like his hero, Leo Peters, and all of a sudden the scales fall from his eyes: *He is Leo Peters*.

Obviously, Leo learns something new when he gets out of his office and looks into the mirror. Something that, by stipulation, he didn't know when he entered his office after the accident, and something he didn't learn from the contents of the box. Could Leo have learned it from the box? It seems we could tell a coherent story in which the box contains all information about Leo there could be and Leo would still not learn from it that the contents in the box are about him. In fact, even seeing himself in the mirror and recognizing that *he* looks like Leo Peters is still compatible with not recognizing that *he* is Leo Peters. Leo is in the same situation as Rudolf Lingens in John Perry's "Frege on Demonstratives":

[6] I am using single quotation marks for mentioning expressions, and double quotation marks, when using a quoted expression.

> An amnesiac, Rudolf Lingens, is lost in Stanford library. He reads a number of things in the library, including a biography of himself, and a detailed account of the library in which he is lost. ... He still won't know who he is and where he is, no matter how much knowledge he piles up, until that moment when he is ready to say,
>
> > *This* place is aisle five, floor six, of Main Library, Stanford. *I* am Rudolf Lingens. (Perry 1977: 492)

Obviously, that Leo learned something new, when he inferred that he is Leo Peters, is not due to the information in the box being in some sense incomplete about Leo. Similarly, the fact that Rudolf Lingens doesn't recognize immediately from his own biography that he is Rudolf Lingens doesn't entail that the biography leaves something out.

Let's consider now a different case. Let's consider the case of Mary, the brilliant color scientist.[7] Mary was raised in a black and white room, and never saw any (other) color in her whole life. Nevertheless, she studied from black and white textbooks and black and white television everything there is to know about color sensation, down to every single neurophysiological detail that occurs when normal-sighted people perceive colors like the color red. One day, Mary is released from her prison and sees for the first time a red tomato. She forms the thought '*This* is what it is like to see red'. Mary clearly learns something new, something she didn't learn in her black and white environment. Does that mean that the information she had access to in her "prison" was incomplete?

Some philosophers think that this is what you should conclude—that the neurophysiological story about color sensation is incomplete and doesn't contain all the relevant facts about color vision and experience, since otherwise Mary couldn't have learned something new when she was released from her "prison". However, after considering the fate of Leo Peters one might be more reluctant to draw this conclusion. After all, Leo learned something new about Leo Peters when he left his office, namely that *he* is Leo Peters, albeit he knew all factual information about Leo Peters already. Perhaps, that's just like what happens to Marry when she learns that *this* is what it is like to see red. Let us look at this case more closely.

2 Zombies and Mary vs. Physicalism

The thought experiment of Mary the color scientist is a thought experiment directed against *physicalism*. Physicalism is a metaphysical doctrine according to which all the common sense mental states, psychological as well as phenomenal, are physical states (Perry 2001B1). What is a physical state?

[7] This thought experiment stems from Frank Jackson and is discussed in (Jackson 1997).

John Perry suggests that it's best to understand these as states that fall under concepts and laws that "suffice in principle for the explanation and prediction of inorganic processes" (Perry 2001B1: 29). Perhaps we can make this idea more precise by defining physical states as those states that are identifiable without reliance on the mental and biological conceptual apparatus: the realm of the inanimate (Papineau 2002: 41).

2.1 A Case for Physicalism

Why should anyone believe that physicalism is true? Perry doesn't present a straightforward argument for physicalism, but rather takes physicalism to be a view he is *prima facie* or "antecedently" convinced of, and which he intends to defend against the "neo-dualist", i.e. the philosopher who claims that there are more properties than those of the inanimate realm; in particular, there are phenomenal states which are not identical with inanimate states.

However, if we look at what Perry takes the "antecedent physicalist" to be subscribing to, it seems that there is a straightforward positive argument for physicalism available. This argument is championed by David Papineau and called the *Causal Argument* (Papineau 2002). Going through it will also help us to better understand what Perry takes his form of physicalism to be committed to.

In its simplest form[8] the *Causal Argument* goes like this:

(C1) Conscious mental events have physical effects.
(C2) All physical effects are fully caused by purely physical prior histories (completeness of physics).
(C3) The physical effects of conscious causes aren't always overdetermined by distinct causes.
(C4) Conclusion: Conscious mental events are identical with some physical causes.

The first premise is a statement of a commonsensical assumption about our mental lives: Sometimes our conscious mental events, and our phenomenal events in particular, cause physical events:

> [P]henomenal states are necessary parts of conditions that causally suffice to make physical things happen. Suppose, for example, that a normal person is sitting in a dentist's chair, with no anesthetic. The dentist drills in such a way as to cause great pain. The pain, together with the connections between the brain and the muscles and such, and a lot of other stuff, caus-

[8] The premises of this argument are quotations from Papineau 2002: 17-18. I merely replaced 'events' for 'occurences' for the sake of terminological continuity with the rest of the discussion.

> ally suffice for the patient to scream, try to grab the drill, and curse the dentist as best as he can with the dentist's drill and the dentist's hands in his mouth. The pain seems to cause the screaming and grasping. It seems that if there were no pain, as there would be had the dentist administered anesthetic, the screaming and grasping would not have occurred. (Perry 2004a: 175)

Of course, we might be in some cases mistaken about the exact causal pathways. Perhaps, sometimes our conscious mental events seem to cause certain physical events, when they in fact just run parallel[9] to events that cause the physical effect in question. But there is no reason to think that we are always or in general mistaken about the causal efficacy of the mental.

The third premise is another, similarly commonsensical assumption about the causal efficacy of the mental. The physical effects that are caused by mental events aren't at the same time sufficiently caused by some distinct inanimate event. In such case, the mental would be causally efficacious, but redundant. Some philosophers (Mellor 1995), defend this so-called "belt and braces" view. They avoid the implausible consequence that I would still have grabbed for the drill, even if I hadn't been in pain, or would still have screamed, even if my neurons hadn't fired, by supposing that there is a strong counterfactual dependence between the respective physical and phenomenal causes that together overdetermine the physical effects in question. But there is no reason to believe the actual world is like this. In fact, nowhere in nature do we find such a mechanism (Papineau 2002).

Perry endorses (C1) in Perry 2001B1 and (C3) in Perry 2004b. Premise (C2), however, is a physical truth. As Papineau (2002) argues, evidence for this premise is relatively recent. It is, on the one hand, supported by the fundamental principle of the conservation of energy in physical systems, and the observation that in physical systems all the apparently contributing forces always reduce to a few basic inanimate forces. On the other hand, premise (C2) receives support from physiological evidence of the last hundred years that there is no sign whatsoever of any non-inanimate forces in any physiological processes. Thus, if Perry takes this premise on board[10], there seems to be a straightforward argument for materialism: Conscious mental states have physical effects, and there is no reason to assume that these causes are redundant. But, since physics is complete, these causes must themselves be physical. Hence, conscious mental states are identical with physical states.

[9] Or in fact happen after the actual cause event.

[10] As he seems to be doing anyway in Perry 2001B1: 79.

This argument supports an identity claim, and Perry emphasizes that he understands physicalism as a type-identity of events. This type-physicalism precludes that "Martians"—beings with a very different physical makeup—can be in the same phenomenal states in which we can be, simply because they can't be in the same physical states. This is a consequence of Perry's view. Some might think that it is an implausible consequence. However, Perry seems ready to bite the bullet. Note that this doesn't preclude that the Martian can be in the same psychological/functional state that we are in when in pain. Moreover, it doesn't preclude that Martians have phenomenal states.

2.2 The Zombie Argument

Physicalism of this kind has often been criticized as being incompatible with some very basic intuitive considerations. One of the most famous arguments against physicalism is perhaps the *Zombie Argument*.[11] The argument goes like this:

(Z1) If two event-types are identical, then it is not possible that they can come apart.

(Z2) We can conceive a possible world in which all physical events take place just as they do in the actual world, but in which no mental events take place.

(Z3) Conceivability implies possibility.

(Z4) Mental event-types are not identical with physical event-types.

The first premise emphasizes the necessity of identity. It is simply not possible for one and the same object, or one and the same state to be distinct from itself.

Premise (Z2) is the result of a thought experiment. Imagine a possible world, physically just like our world, but without any phenomenal states. There are doppelgangers of you and me, who act and move in exactly the same way as we do, but without thereby being in any phenomenal state. There is nothing it is like to be such a "zombie"-doppelganger. When my zombie-twin goes to the zombie-dentist, he will also scream, try to grab the drill, and curse the dentist as best as he can with the dentist's drill and the dentist's hands in his mouth, just as I do; however, my zombie-twin will not be in pain when he is doing this—he will not feel anything at all.

If this is conceivable, and if conceivability implies possibility (premise (Z3)), then it seems that it is possible that phenomenal states and physical states come apart. But then physical and phenomenal states can't be identical, not even in this world.

---

[11] The *Zombie Argument* goes back to (Kirk 1974a and 1974b).

2.3 Is the Zombie Argument Question Begging?

Perry argues that there is no reason for the physicalist to accept the zombie-scenario as conceivable.[12] He argues that the *Zombie Argument* presupposes epiphenomenalism. Remember, what the *Zombie Argument* asks us to do: imagine a possible world, *physically just like ours*. Well, in our world, phenomenal states have physical effects, or at least this is what the physicalist, who denies epiphenomenalism, is committed to. But if phenomenal states in our world cause physical effects, and if a zombie world is supposed to be physically just like ours, then in the zombie world either (a) something else must cause these physical effects, (b) these physical effects occur uncaused, or (c) these physical effects don't occur. If (c) then the zombie world is not physically like our world. Consider the dentist episode again: In our world grabbing and screaming occurs, partly caused by the pain that the drilling causes. The grabbing and screaming is part of what is going on physically in our world; if it is missing in the physical world, then the zombie world is physically discernible from our world.

If (b) then, again, the zombie world is physically discernible from our world, since in our world these physical effects do not occur uncaused.

(a) could be the case if all physical effects that are caused by phenomenal states are always overdetermined (such that there is always also a sufficient physical cause) in the actual world; *or* (a) could be the case because other physical causes are present in the zombie-world and replace the actual phenomenal causes. Of course, the latter option violates again the requirement that the zombie world is supposed to be physically indiscernible from our world. The former option, however, we have already discussed above when considering premise (C3) of the *Causal Argument*. There we said that there is no reason to assume that this kind of overdetermination occurs in the actual world. Note, moreover, that the sophisticated "belt and braces" view, discussed above, which supposes that there is a strong counterfactual dependence between the respective physical and phenomenal causes that together overdetermine the physical effects in question, wouldn't help the zombie world: If this counterfactual dependence is a fact about the physical back-up causes in our world, then this physical fact must be missing in the zombie world, or else the physical cause wouldn't be there if the phenomenal cause wasn't, and hence, again, the zombie world can't physically be like our world.[13]

---

[12] Or, to be more precise, to accept it as conceivable in a way that would be required for conceivability to imply possibility (as premise (Z4) requires).

[13] For a discussion of whether and how the *Zombie Argument* presupposes epiphenomenalism, see Bailey 2006 and 2009.

It is not clear, though, whether Perry's defense against the *Zombie Argument* ultimately works. After all, many non-epiphenomenalist materialists find zombies conceivable (see Chalmers 2004a for a discussion). Moreover, there is a nearby argument that is not as easy to rebut, the *Inverted Spectrum Argument*:

(I1) If two event-types are identical, then it is not possible that they can come apart.
(I2) We can conceive a possible world in which all physical events take place just as they do in the actual world, but in which the mental events causing them are systematically inverted.
(I3) Conceivability implies possibility.
(I4) Mental event-types are not identical with physical event-types.

Here all premises are as they were in the *Zombie Argument*, but we change the second premise and the accompanying thought experiment. Imagine a possible world in which, say, your color experiences are systematically inverted. Whenever you actually experience something as red in the actual world, you there experience it as blue. Imagine also that in this world all physical effects of the phenomenal states accompanying your color experiences remain the same as they are in the actual world (just with inverted causes).

Such a world doesn't presuppose epiphenomenalism, since also in the twin world the relevant physical effects have phenomenal causes. Is this world physically like our world? Perry *says* it is not:

> [N]ot only must the physical facts involved with language and observable behavior be held constant, and not only the functions of the color sensations, but all the physical facts that are in any way relevant to color experience, down to the finest details in the rods and cones—the place where the differences in color experiences that we know of have their origin—and beyond, including events in the visual cortex and anywhere else relevant to vision and the experience of it. ... [W]e can grant ... [that] we have twins with color experiences systematically inverted relative to our own, and these inversions do not lead to any differences in linguistic or other behavior. But there is no reason to grant ... the second requirement: that some of these worlds are physically indiscernible from our own. If the antecedent physicalist is right, none will be. (Perry 2001B1: 91)

Of course, if the antecedent physicalist is right, then such a possibility would be excluded, but this just begs the question against the neo-dualist. After all, the argument reasons *if inverted spectra in physical duplicate worlds are possible, then physicalism is false*. Pointing out that inverted spectra are impossible if physicalism is true, is not providing a counterargument.[14]

It seems that Perry's strategy to reject the conceivability of the relevant scenario doesn't work for the *Inverted Spectrum Argument*. It is true that Perry subscribes to "antecedent physicalism", which means that he is entitled to assume that physicalism is true and may, on that assumption, point out what would make a purported conceivable scenario inconceivable after all. In the zombie case he can do that by pointing out that a zombie world can't be conceived as being physically indiscernible from the actual world, unless one believes that epiphenomenalism is actually true. However, in the inverted spectrum case, the prima facie conceivability is not conflicting with any particular bit of physical knowledge or any other bit of the antecedent physicalist's assumptions about the actual world. True, it conflicts with the assumption that physicalism is true, but I'm afraid that this maneuver doesn't help Perry's case, as it reminds too much of a joke David Lewis once told:

> Mr. Z claims to have found a counterexample to my theory. But he has misunderstood me, he has not interpreted my words as I intended. For I intended that there be no counterexamples. (Lewis 1984: 221)

Unless Perry can point to something in the inverted spectrum scenario that is incompatible with what the antecedent physicalist believes the physical world is like, rejecting the inverted spectrum world as inconceivable, because it's possibility would conflict with physicalism, simply begs the question against the neo-dualist.

Fortunately, Perry has other resources to attack the third premise of the *Zombie Argument* and the *Inverted Spectrum Argument*. The strategy he eventually uses to block that premise is the same that he also adopts to block the *Knowledge Argument*, i.e. the argument based on the thought experiment with Mary the color scientist, whom we met above.

2.4 The Knowledge Argument

The *Knowledge Argument* goes like this:

(K1) If physicalism is true, then all facts are physical facts.

(K2) If all facts are physical facts, then knowing all the physical facts is knowing all the facts.

---

[14] Note that Perry's reply to the *Zombie Argument* is not begging the question in this way. There the argument isn't that a zombie world couldn't be a physical duplicate world, because qualia are physical states. The argument is that qualia have physical effects in the actual world, and that the physical facts in the actual world are such that these effects aren't already caused by all (other) physical states, if we take the phenomenal states away. Unfortunately, Perry himself is not always clear on this matter (cf. Perry 2001 B1: 77, last paragraph of 4.1).

(K3) Mary learns something new when she leaves the black and white room.
(K4) Mary knew all the physical facts.
(K5) Her new knowledge is knowledge of a fact that existed prior to Mary's leaving the room.
(K6) If Mary learns something new when leaving the room, her new knowledge is of a fact, and if she knew all the physical facts, then there are facts that are not physical facts.
(K7) Therefore, physicalism is false.

(K1) is a more general statement of the claim the physicalist wishes to defend. Physicalism just is the view that all facts are physical facts. But if that is the case, then (K2) is a triviality: if all facts are physical facts, then knowing all the physical facts is knowing all the facts. (K3) follows from the thought experiment we told above. Mary is a brilliant color scientist who learns everything there is to know about the physical world, including everything physical there is to know about color experiences. However, when she exits her black and white prison and sees for the first time a ripe tomato, she learns what it is like to see red:

> And this is something new, something she didn't know and couldn't have predicted, in spite of knowing all the relevant physical facts. She learns what it is like to have a certain experience, the experience of seeing red. (Perry 2001B1: 94)

It is important to get clear on what (kind of) knowledge it is that Mary acquires. There are at least two important questions that need to be answered: (i) Is Mary's new knowledge *knowledge that* or *knowledge how*? (ii) Is Mary's new knowledge of a fact that already existed when she was in the black and white room, or is it knowledge of a new fact?

Let's consider the second question first. Here it is important how the new knowledge gets reported. When Mary leaves her prison, she has a new experience. Perry (2001B1: 95) considers three candidates for the new knowledge that Mary acquires at that moment:

(1) This is what it is like to have my present experience.
(2) This is what it is like for me now to see red.
(3) This is what it is like to see red.

The first of these is something that Mary certainly learns for the first time when she leaves the room. However, this new knowledge can't pose a threat for the physicalist, since it is knowledge of a fact that just came into existence when she left the room. There is no way she could have known (1) before she actually had that experience, because there wasn't anything of this sort for her to know about. (2) is something that she is now in a position to infer given (1) and her knowledge that ripe tomatoes are red, but it is, likewise, merely knowledge of a new fact. What makes Mary's new knowledge problematic for the physicalist is the fact that she learns something about red experiences in general, not merely about red experiences of her own, or red experiences that she is having right now. (3) seems to capture this new knowledge as it is relevant for the *Knowledge Argument*.

> (3) was true before Mary had her experience. So if (3) is a physical fact, it could have been and should have been included in the texts Mary read in her black and white room, and she should already know it. Normal red-seeing was something she was to know all about in the black and white room. But she doesn't already know it. So it wasn't included in what she read. So it isn't a physical fact. That's the problem. (Perry 2001B1: 97)

Let's now turn to question (i), what kind of knowledge is it that Mary acquires? It is customary to distinguish between "knowledge that" and "knowledge how". The former is propositional knowledge, knowledge of a fact, that (at least typically) can be put into and learned from a description. Knowledge how, is, however, the possession of an ability that might(!) not be communicable at all. Laurence Nemirow (1990) argues that knowing what it's like to see a color should be identified with the ability to visualize the color. Thus, the knowledge that Mary gains when leaving the black and white room is the ability to visualize the color red. Nemirow calls the identification of knowing what it's like with knowing how to imagine the "ability equation":

> The more seriously we take this ability equation, the easier it becomes to resist the knowledge argument. The latter assumes that science cannot convey what it's like to see red. The premise is uncontentious, for science does not seek to instill imaginative abilities. But the knowledge argument concludes that physical science cannot describe certain information about seeing red. The inference is invalid because it presumes that knowing what it's like is propositional knowledge rather than an ability. (Nemirow 1990, 493)

Nemirow argues that the ability equation is "confirmed by its explanatory power". In particular, it can account for three facts that otherwise threaten to undermine physicalism: (i) The ability equation explains why it is appropriate to use the vocabulary of knowledge ("discovering", "knowing", "forgetting", etc.) when discussing what an experience is like; (ii) it accounts for the subjectivity of experience, the fact that only those that can have certain experiences can know what they are like, by simply identifying the two conditions; and (iii) it accounts for the linguistic inexpressibility of knowing what it is like, since some abilities (like the ability to wiggle your ears, or the ability to ride a bicycle) are inexpressible. If Nemirow is right, and Mary's new knowledge isn't propositional knowledge, then the *Knowl-*

edge Argument breaks down, since it can't establish that Mary's new knowledge is knowledge of a *fact* left out by a comprehensive account of all the physical facts.

But it is not clear that Nemirow's response works. Perry, in any case, is persuaded by arguments offered by Brian Loar (1990) and Bill Lycan (1995) that knowledge what it is like is indeed propositional knowledge. Perry explicitly endorses Loar's argument that some of our phenomenal knowledge is of a logical form that does not allow being analyzed as a mere ability. Take embeddings like 'If apples hadn't looked like *this*, I would have found them more attractive', where '*this*' is Mary's way of thinking of the looks of apples in terms of her experientially based concept. 'Looks like this' is introducing, in Loar's words, a predicate with a distinctive content, and doesn't merely express the possession of Mary's recognitional know-how.[15]

Taking these considerations together, we seem to have to endorse (K5). We said that Mary's knowledge is propositional, hence knowledge of a fact, and the fact is one that was already there to be known before Mary left the black and white room. (K4) simply follows from stipulations in the thought experiment. But then (K6) just seems to be trivial and should lead us to conclude (K7): Physicalism is false, not all facts are physical facts.

2.5 The Modal Argument

The *Modal Argument* goes back to Saul Kripke's discussion of physicalism in his "Naming and Necessity" (1980). Before that, philosophers who advocated the identity-theory between mind and body or between sensations and brain processes, described their view as defending a "contingent" identity. J. J. C. Smart's "Sensations and Brain Processes" (1959) provides a famous example of this view:

> When I say that a sensation is a brain process or that lightning is electric discharge, I am using "is" in the sense of strict identity. ... [T]here can be contingent statements of the form "A is identical with B," and a person may well know that something is an A without knowing that it is a B. An illiterate peasant might well be able to talk about his sensations without knowing about his brain processes, just as he can talk about lightning though he knows nothing of electricity. (Smart 1959: 145–47)

Kripke argued that such a view is confused. Even if statements of the form 'A is identical with B' might sometimes be a posteriori, they can't be contingent if 'A' and 'B' are rigid designators. A "rigid designator" is an expression (like, for example, a proper name) that refers to the same object in every possible world in which that object exists. Now, since one and the

[15] One might consider this as the Frege-Geach problem turned on the ability hypothesis.

same thing can't be two different things in another possible world, identity statements with rigid designators flanking the identity sign can't be contingent. The only way for an identity statement to be false at another possible world is if the terms in the identity statement refer to something else in that world.

One might think that this is not yet a problem for the physicalist. Perhaps physicalists have just been at bit careless in stating their position. Instead of claiming that the identity statement they are defending is "contingent", they should have said that it is *a posteriori*—they just conflated a modal with an epistemological notion.[16] And that the identity is a posteriori should be okay to say, since this is just what seems to be the right thing to say about 'Water is H_2O' or 'Heat is molecular motion', which, according Kripke, are also necessary truths (in virtue of rigid designation), but could only be discovered a posteriori to be true.

Kripke argues, however, that this is not a move the physicalist can make either. Let us take as our example the type-identity thesis that Kripke discusses: 'having pain is having ones C-fibers firing' or

(P) pain = C-fiber firing

As the antecedent physicalist is ready to admit, (P) is conceivably false. We can imagine creatures in pain without their C-fibers firing as well as we can imagine beings like us with firing C-fibers that aren't in pain. However, this is no problem, since

(H) heat = molecular motion

is likewise conceivably false. We can imagine heat being something other than molecular motion. If we couldn't, we could have figured out (H) a priori, but it required empirical research to discover that (H) is true.

But here Kripke disagrees. (H) expresses a necessary identity. Hence (H) isn't possibly false. When we conceive (H) to be false, we aren't imagining a possible world in which heat isn't molecular motion, but a possible world where something other than molecular motions, and thus *something other than heat* causes heat-sensations in the beings at this world. The contingency of (H) is merely apparent. We can explain it away by presenting a possible world that is qualitatively like our world and that we confused with a world in which heat isn't molecular motion.

But, although this is the right thing to say about (H), we can't say the same about (P). In order to explain the apparent contingency of (P) away,

[16] If you read the quote from J. J. C. Smart again, this is precisely what seems to be going on. Smart wants to grant that the illiterate peasant doesn't *know* that his sensations are brain processes, and he expresses this by granting that the identity in question is contingent.

we also would need to be able to present a possible world that we confused for a world in which (P) is false. If we follow the example of (H) this should be a possible world where pain is dissociated from our qualitative experiencing pain. Just like in the case of (H), where we explained away the appearance of contingency by presenting a world in which heat is molecular motion, but something else causes heat-sensations, we now need to present a world in which pain is C-fiber firing, but something else causes pain-sensations. But such a world is impossible to present. If something feels like pain, it *is* pain. There is no way to dissociate pain from pain-sensations in the way we can dissociate heat from heat-sensations. But this delivers another argument against antecedent physicalism:

(M1) 'pain' and 'C-fiber-firing' are rigid designators.
(M2) A true identity statement with two rigid designators is necessarily true.
(M3) In order to explain away a conceivable world as merely apparently possible, we need to present a possible world, the qualitative features of which can explain our mistake.
(M4) It is conceivable that pain is not C-fiber-firing.
(M5) It is impossible to present a possible world in which there are pain-sensations, but no pain.
(M6) Therefore, 'pain = C-fiber firing' is false.

How can the antecedent physicalist respond to these challenges?

3 Reflexive Content and the Subject Matter Fallacy

Perry thinks that the *Knowledge Argument* and the *Modal Argument* are based on the same mistake, they both commit the *subject-matter fallacy*. In both cases we are presented with certain epistemic possibilities: in the Mary case the possibilities that Mary rules out when she learns something new, in the *Modal Argument*, the possibilities that account for the conceivability of (P) being false. Both arguments arrive at their conclusion (i.e. that physicalism is false) by locating these possibilities in the "subject matter": They are possibilities concerning qualitative experience, the subject matter that Mary learns something new about, respectively, the subject matter (P) is about. Why is this a fallacy?

To see Perry's point, we need to introduce his notion of *reflexive content*. Take the (official) content of my belief that John Perry is the author of "Knowledge, Possibility, and Consciousness". In Perry's usage, the subject matter of that belief are the things and conditions the belief is about: John Perry, the book "Knowledge, Possibility, and Consciousness," and the relation of being the author of. Thus, the proposition *that John Perry is the author of "Knowledge, Possibility, and Consciousness*," is naturally taken to be the content of my belief. But, Perry emphasizes, this isn't *the* content of my belief, it's only the content of my belief given certain facts about reference. If these are in place and fixed, then the subject matter of my belief becomes at the same time the relevant content (Perry 2003b). Perry makes the point with the help of a formula he calls the "Content Analyzer":

(CA) Given *such and such*, φ is true iff *so and so*.

φ is any truth-evaluable representation, *such and such* are facts about φ, and *so and so* is the content of φ given those facts (Perry 2003b: 97). Thus *so and so*, is the additional or (in Perry's terminology) *incremental* content of φ, given *such and such*. This content might vary, when we vary what is given. How variation in these conditions affects the content is best explained with an example:

> Consider Donnellan's famous example, "Smith's murderer is insane". Given that the statement is in English, the facts about its syntax and the meanings of its words, what *else* has to be the case for it to be true? There must be a unique individual that murdered Smith, and that individual must be insane. This is the "attributive content". Now suppose we add to what is given the fact that Jones murdered Smith. Then what *else* must be the case for the statement to be true? Jones must be insane. This is the "referential content" in Donnellan's terminology. I shall say that the facts about the designation of "Smith's murderer" were *loaded* in the latter case, and *unloaded* in the former. (Perry 2003b: 97)

The representation φ is the statement 'Smith's murderer is insane', in the first case, we fix the *such and such*-conditions to the statement's being in English, it's syntax, and the meaning of its words, and we arrive at the *so and so*-conditions that have to be satisfied for φ to be true. These *so and so*-conditions change, if we load more into the *such and such*-conditions. If all the facts about φ are fixed, including the meanings and referents of the words that occur in it and the context of utterance, CA gives us the *referential content* of φ. Although the latter is what we are often interested in, it is often not very useful when we want to explain the cognitive significance of statements. Let's assume (to adapt Perry's favorite example), that I read "Knowledge, Possibility, and Consciousness," and know that

I. John Perry wrote "Knowledge, Possibility, and Consciousness".

At an APA meeting I meet this very amicable, very funny guy, who seems to also be interested in philosophy of mind and philosophy of language, and I tell him about "Knowledge, Possibility, and Consciousness" and how it changed my life and my thinking about consciousness, content, and chocolate chip cookies. To my embarrassment, it turns out that the amicable guy I'm talking to is John Perry himself.

II. That man (I'm talking to) wrote "Knowledge, Possibility, and Consciousness".

(I.) and (II.) have the same referential content. However, obviously I learn something new, when I come to realize (II.), something I didn't know already from knowing (I.). The Content Analyzer can help us to appreciate their difference:

III. Given that (I.) is in English, etc., (I.) is true iff the person the speaker of (I.) is using 'John Perry' to refer to is the author of "Knowledge, Possibility, and Consciousness".

IV. Given that (II.) is in English, etc., (II.) is true iff the person the speaker of (II.) is attending to and drawing attention to is the author of "Knowledge, Possibility, and Consciousness".

The contents are "reflexive", since the analyzed statements themselves occur in the right-hand side of the biconditional that is specifying the truth conditions. These reflexive contents aren't part of the subject matter of these statements; likewise, if (I.) or (II.) are reports of my beliefs, their reflexive contents are not what I believe. However, the Content Analyzer tells us, which cognitive significance a statement or a belief might have for an individual and how the statement or belief might play a role for perception and action.

Most of this, I take it, should be familiar to you from the previous chapters. Let's see how it helps the antecedent physicalist to answer the *Knowledge Argument* and the *Modal Argument*.

3.1 What Mary Learns

Let's return to Mary first. When she is in the black and white room, she learns all there is to know about color-perception. We suppose that the neuroscience textbooks that Mary is using in her studies have all the subjective characters of subjective experience systematically named, and 'Q_R' is defined as the subjective character people with normal vision see when they look at a red object under normal light conditions. Thus Mary knows from her black and white room[17]

(1) Q_R is what it's like to see red.

When she leaves the black and white room she sees red for the first time. She is attending to the subjective character of her experience in a subjective way and uses the inner demonstrative label 'this$_i$' to communicate what she is noticing and learning when leaving the black and white room for the first time and seeing a ripe tomato:

[17] The following example sentences, (1)-(6), are quoted from Perry 2001B1: 146–48.

(2) This$_i$ is what it is like to see red.
(3) Q_R is this$_i$ subjective character.

Let us label the beliefs that correspond to (1), (2), and (3), 'b_1', 'b_2', and 'b_3'. Perry argues that the following can all be true together (Perry 2001B1: 146-147):

- Q_R is a physical state, a physical aspect of the normal experience of seeing red.
- (1), (2), and (3) are true.
- When Mary leaves the Jackson room she learns something new, by forming the new true beliefs b_2 and b_3, that she expresses with (2) and (3).

The new knowledge she gains is recognitional or identificational knowledge, which is the same in kind as the knowledge I gain in the story above when I realize at the APA meeting that the guy I'm talking to is John Perry. With the help of the Content Analyzer, we can see this at the level of reflexive truth conditions:

(4) b_1 is true iff the origin of Mary's Q_R concept, the concept involved in b_1, is the subjective character of the experience of seeing red.
(5) b_2 is true iff the act of inner attention to which it is attached is of the subjective character of the experience of seeing red.
(6) b_3 is true iff the act of inner attention to which it is attached is of the origin of Mary's Q_R concept.

Although the subject matter content of (1), (2), and (3) is the same, their reflexive contents are different. b_1 was, in Perry's terminology, a *detached* belief, like my belief that Perry wrote "Knowledge, Possibility, and Consciousness" that I had before I met Perry at the APA. It is not connected to any experience of the subjective character of seeing red, like my belief about Perry isn't connected to any perception of Perry. b_2 is analogous to the belief I acquire at the APA, when Perry introduces himself to me.

b_3 is the belief that seemed to cause trouble for the physicalist. This is what Mary should have known already on the basis of knowing all the physical facts. Now we see that at the level of subject matter content, Mary knew it all along. What she learns does not show at the level of truth conditions for her beliefs given what they refer to. What Mary learns all happens at the level of reflexive truth conditions.

> Given that subjective aspects are physical aspects, they can in principle be observed, discussed, and written up in textbooks. So people can learn about subjective characters that they have never had. They can know of

> subjective characters they have never experienced, that they are the subjective characters normally associated with certain kinds of experience, such as seeing red. All of this does not mean that the antecedent physicalist needs to deny that a person in this position, such as Mary, learns something new when she does finally experience the subjective character in question. The new knowledge … is found at the level of reflexive content. (Perry 2001B1: 149–50)

This shows how our introductory story about Leo Peters is analogous to Mary's story in the black and white room. When Leo recognizes that he is Leo Peters, he immediately gains a lot of new knowledge much of which he had lost due to his accident, some of which he had forgotten already before. For example, he knows now that *he* went to Ridgemont High School. He knew, before he looked in the mirror, that Leo Peters went to Ridgemont High; the subject matter, the *referential* content, of both beliefs is the same: What Leo learns needs to be analyzed at the level of reflexive content, just like Mary's new knowledge.

3.2 Rebutting the Modal Argument

It might be obvious now how Perry rebuts the *Modal Argument*. The *Modal Argument* asks us to eliminate an open epistemic possibility, and since we can't explain this possibility away as a misdescribed real possibility, the argument concludes that the possibility in question is a subject matter possibility, in conflict with the truth of physicalism.

Again, Perry's strategy is to present the possibility in question at the level of reflexive content. We were looking for a way to explain the apparent contingency of

(P) pain = C-fiber firing.

According to Perry, the possibility that explains the apparent contingency of this necessary truth, is the possibility that the two concepts, our concept of pain and our concept of C-fiber firing, do not co-refer.

The *Modal Argument* suggests that this move is blocked: Our phenomenal pain concept (the core of which is what Perry calls our "Humean idea of pain") necessarily refers to the state of pain, because there is nothing else it could fit. Likewise does our concept of C-fibre firing rigidly refer to the state of pain via its essential scientific properties. There is no way these two couldn't co-refer, if they do. Perry objects that this is the wrong analysis. It is true that our Humean idea of pain necessarily *fits* only the state of pain. It is also true that the scientific concept of C-fiber firing *describes* the state of pain by its essential scientific properties. However, this does not establish that the two terms co-refer.

Reference, according to Perry, is a matter "of the circumstantial facts that determine source and applicandum" (Perry 2001B1: 185). My concept of pain refers rigidly to pain because pain experiences are the source of this concept. That my pain concept also fits the experience it is of (and nothing else) doesn't matter for reference. Here is an example involving smells:

> For most of us, our memories of smells are much less distinctive, and more easily confused one with the other, than our ideas of colors, or of different kinds of severe pains. Suppose over the years of a spice-deprived life, I have come to think that cinnamon and nutmeg are the same spice, and the smell of cinnamon and nutmeg are the same, and the sensation of smelling cinnamon and the sensation of smelling nutmeg are the same. I experienced both in childhood but not since. I have not had another chance to smell them. When I am given a chance to experience these smells again, I at once recognize my mistake. The new experiences enrich the old ideas; I know at a sniff, which is nutmeg and which is cinnamon, and how different they are. But before that I conceived that they were the same—the spices, the smells, and the sensations. (Perry 2004a: 179–80)

In this story, Perry has two concepts with two Humean ideas, one idea of the smell of cinnamon, the other of the smell of nutmeg. Both concepts are rigid designators: They rigidly refer to the smells that gave rise to them, and they continue to do so even when Perry has forgotten that they are of two different smells. Thus Perry's belief, that the sensation of smelling nutmeg is the same as the sensation of smelling cinnamon, is false in every possible world. But then, what world gets excluded when Perry sniffs these smells again and recognizes his mistake? Again, the answer lies in the reflexive content of the belief. The possibility in question is one in which the source of Perry's phenomenal concept of what it is like to smell nutmeg is the same as the source of Perry's phenomenal concept of what it is like to smell cinnamon. Likewise might a scientific concept happen to denote stimulated C-fibers, although something else is the source of that concept (Perry 2001B1: 186).

Thus, although (P) doesn't follow the example of (H), the identification of heat with molecular motion, because our concept of pain, unlike our concept of heat, is *direct* (we don't experience pain by experiencing something that is caused by pain) we can nevertheless find the possibility that explains the apparent contingency of (P) at the level of reflexive content.

4 Conclusions?

In this chapter we have seen how Perry uses his logico-sematic apparatus to rebut some of the most forceful arguments against physicalism. For reasons of space we couldn't look into Perry's reply to David Chalmers' version of the *Modal Argument*. For the full story, one should consult Perry 2001B1 and 2004b, as well as Chalmers' response (Chalmers 2004a and 2004b).

It is probably unsurprising that this isn't the last word in the dualism-debate. There are at least two kinds of worries one might have about Perry's solution. One type concerns the satisfactoriness of the semantic framework, the other whether the proposed responses to the *Modal Argument* and the *Knowledge Argument* are ultimately successful. Since the semantic framework has been discussed in other chapters of this book, I will only raise one worry of the latter type. It concerns the stubbornness of the intuition that pain could be dissociated from the physical state it correlates with. Typically, when we learn that *A* is identical with *B*, we don't find it conceivable anymore that *A* could be dissociated from *B*. However, our dualist intuition seems to survive our physicalist insights. One might hope for an explanation here too.

Perry *can* explain why (P) isn't a priori, by pointing out that our phenomenological concept of pain "is not introduced, explicitly or implicitly, in terms of the concepts of brain science" (Perry 2001B1: 187). But it is not just the non a priority of (P) that needs explaining, but also the continuing intuition that (P) might have been false even after we know that it is true, which seems to be absent in other cases of informative identities.[18]

Acknowledgements

I would like to thank Bruno Mölder for helpful comments on an earlier draft of this paper. I would also like to acknowledge the support of the Estonian Science Foundation, projects SFLFI11085E and SF0180110s08.

[18] For a discussion of this problem see Papineau 2002.

Perry's Philosophical Works and Further References

Perry's Philosophical Works

Books

1978B. *A Dialogue on Personal Identity and Immortality*. Indianapolis: Hackett Publishing Company.

1983B. *Situations and Attitudes*. With J. Barwise. Cambridge, Mass.: MIT Press. (Reprinted with a new introduction, Stanford: CSLI 1999)

1993B. *The Problem of the Essential Indexical and Other Essays*. New York: Oxford University Press. (Enlarged ed.: Stanford: CSLI 2000)

1999B1. *Problems d'Indexicalité*. Selected Essays by J. Dokic and F. Preisig. Stanford/Paris: CSLI.

1999B2. *Dialogue on Good, Evil and the Existence of God*. Cambridge/Indianapolis: Hackett.

2001B1. *Knowledge, Possibility and Consciousness*. Cambridge, Mass.: MIT Press.

2001B2. *Reference and Reflexivity*. Stanford: CSLI.

2002B1. *Identity, Personality and the Self*. Indianapolis: Hackett.

2002B2. *Contesti*. Genova: De Ferrari & Devega.

2011B. *Critical Pragmatics. An Inquiry into Reference and Communication*. With Kepa Korta. Cambridge, Mass: Cambridge University Press.

Books Edited

1975E. *Personal Identity*. Berkeley: University of California Press.

1985E. *Introduction to Philosophy*, ed. J. Perry and M. Bratman. New York: Oxford University Press. (Revised ed.: 1993. 3rd ed.: 1999. 4th ed.: 2006, ed. J. Perry, M. Bratman, and J. Fischer)

1989E. *Themes from Kaplan*. With J. Among and H. Wettstein. New York: Oxford University Press.

1990E. *Situation Theory and Its Applications*. Vol. 1. With R. Cooper and K. Mukai. Stanford: CSLI Publications.

1994E. *Berkeley's Three Dialogue*. With D. Hilbert. Claremont: Arete Press.

Articles

1963. Paradoxical Logic. *Philosophy East and West* 13:155–7.

1967. Equality and Education: Remarks on Kleinberger. *Studies in Philosophy and Education* V:433–45.

1970a. The Same F. *The Philosophical Review* 79:181–200. (Reprinted in Perry 2002B1)

1970b. Review of Cornman and Lehrer, *Philosophical Problems and Arguments*. *Philosophical Review* 97:578–80.

1970c. Review of David Wiggins, *Identity and Spatial Temporal Continuity*. *Journal of Symbolic Logic* 35:447–8.

1972. Can The Self Divide? *Journal of Philosophy* 69:463–88. (Reprinted in Perry 2002B1)

1974a. Review of *Three Paradoxical Aspects of Identity*, by Heinrich Behmann. *Journal of Symbolic Logic* 39:359–60

1974b. Review of *Universals*, by Nicholas Wolterstorff. *Journal of Philosophy*. 71:252–7.

1975a. The Problem of Personal Identity. *Personal Identity*, ed. J. Perry, 3–31. Berkeley: University of California Press.

1975b. Personal Identity, Memory, and the Problem of Circularity. *Personal Identity*, ed. J. Perry, 135–157. Berkeley: University of California Press. (Reprinted in Perry 2002B1)

1975c. Reviews of Gustav Bergmann, *Sameness, Meaning, and Identity*, and Gustav Bergmann and Herbert Hochberg, *Concepts*. *Journal of Symbolic Logic* 40:106-7.

1976a. Review of Bernard Williams, *Problems of the Self*. *Journal of Philosophy* 73:416–28.

1976b. The Importance of Being Identical. *The Identity of Persons*, ed. A. Rorty. Berkeley: University of California Press. (Reprinted in Perry 2002B1)

1977. Frege on Demonstratives. *Philosophical Review* 86:474–97. (Reprinted in Perry, J. 1993B)

1978a. A Dialogue on Personal Identity and Immortality. *Reason and Responsibility*, ed. J. Feinberg. 4th ed. Encino, Calif.: Dickenson Publishing Company. (Reprinted with revisions as Perry 1978B)

1978b. Relative Identity and Relative Number. *Canadian Journal of Philosophy* 7:1–14. (Reprinted in Perry 2002B1)

1978c. Defenses for the Mind-Brain Identity Theory: Commentary on Puccetti and Dykes. *The Behavioral and Brain Sciences* 1:362

1979a. The Problem of the Essential Indexical. Noûs 13:3–21. (Reprinted in *The Philosophers Annual*, III, 1980)

1979b. The Philosophical Problem of Personal Identity. *Stanford Observer*, March 1979:3–4.

1980a. Belief and Acceptance. *Midwest Studies in Philosophy* 5:533–42. (Reprinted Perry 1993B.)

1980b. A Problem about Continued Belief. *Pacific Philosophical Quarterly* 61:317–22. (Reprinted in Perry 1993B)

1980c. The Situation Underground. With J. Barwise. *Stanford Working Papers in Semantics*, ed. J. Barwise and I. Sag. Vol. I. Stanford: Stanford Cognitive Science Group.

1981a. Semantic Innocence and Uncompromising Situations. With J. Barwise. *Midwest Studies in Philosophy* 6:387–403.

1981b. Will Tommy Vladek Survive? *Thought Probes: An Introduction to Philosophy Through Science Fiction*, ed. F. D. Miller and N. D. Smith. Englewood Cliffs, NJ: Prentice-Hall.

1981c. Situations and Attitudes. With J. Barwise. *Journal of Philosophy* 77:668–91.

1983a. Castañeda on He and I. *Agent, Language, and World: Essays Presented to Hector-Neri Castañeda with his Replies*, ed. J. E. Tomberlin. Indianapolis: Hackett Publishing Company. (Reprinted in Perry 1993B)

1983b. Personal Identity and the Concept of a Person. *Chronicles of Institut International De Philosophie. Volume IV, Philosophy of Mind* (*Philosophy: A New Survey*), ed. G. Floistad. The Hague: Martinus Nijhoff. (Reprinted in Perry 2002B1)

1983c. Contradictory Situations. *Varieties of Formal Semantics: Proceedings of the 4th Amsterdam Colloquium, September, 1982*, ed. F. Landmann and F. Veltman. Dordrecht: Foris.

1985a. Shifting Situations and Shaken Attitudes. With J. Barwise. *Linguistics and Philosophy* 8:105–61. (Also Report No. CSLI-84-13. Stanford University: Center for the Study of Language and Information, 1984. Reprinted in the augmented edition of Perry 1983B in 1999)

1985b. Language, Mind, and Information. *Report of Workshop on Information and Representation*, ed. B. H. Partee, S. Peters, and R. Thomason. (Also Report No. CSLI-85-44. Stanford University: Center for the Study of Language and Information, 1985.)

1985c. Self-Knowledge and Self-Representation. *Proceedings of IJCAI-1985*. Mountain View: Morgan Kaufmann.

1985d. Semantics. *The Social Science Encyclopedia*, ed. A. Kuper and J. Kuper. London: Routledge and Kegan Paul.

1986a. Perception, Action, and the Structure of Believing. *Philosophical Grounds of Rationality*, ed. R. E. Grandy and R. Warner. Oxford: Oxford University Press. (Reprinted in Perry 1993B)

1986b. Circumstantial Attitudes and Benevolent Cognition. *Language, Mind and Logic*, ed. J. Butterfield. Cambridge: Cambridge University Press. (Also Report No. CSLI-86-53, Stanford University: Center for the Study of Language and Information, 1986. Reprinted in Perry 1993B.)

1986c. From Worlds to Situations. *Journal of Philosophical Logic* 15:83–107. (Reprinted in Perry 1993B)

1986d. Thought without Representation. *Supplementary Proceedings of the Aristotelian Society* 60:137–51. (Reprinted in Perry 1993B, 205–218. 2nd ed.: 2000, 171–188)

1988a. Cognitive Significance and New Theories of Reference. *Noûs* 2:1–18. (Reprinted in Perry 1993B)

1988b. Review of *A Border Dispute*, by John MacNamara. *Cognition*, 30:183–188.

1989a. Possible Worlds and Subject Matter: Discussion of Barbara H. Partee's 'Possible Worlds in Model-Theoretic Semantics: A Linguistic Perspective'. *Possible Worlds in Humanities, Arts and Sciences: Proceedings of Nobel Symposium, August, 1986, 65*, ed. S. Allen. Berlin/New York: Walter de Gruyter. (Reprinted in Perry 1993B)

1989b. The Prince and the Phonebooth: Reporting Puzzling Beliefs. With Mark Crimmins. *Journal of Philosophy* 86:685–711. (Also Report No. CSLI-88-128. Stanford University: Center for the Study of Language and Information, 1988. Reprinted in *The Philosophers Annual*, XII, 1989 and in Perry 1993B: 249–77. 2nd ed.: 2000, 207–32).

1990a. What is Information? With D. Israel. *Information, Language and Cognition*, ed. P. Hanson. Vancouver: University of British Columbia Press.

1990b. Individuals in Informational and Intentional Content. *Information, Semantics and Epistemology*, ed. E. Villanueva. Oxford: Blackwell. (Reprinted in Perry 1993B)

1990c. Self-Notions. *Logos* 11:17–31.

1991a. Fodor and Psychological Explanations. With D. Israel. *Meaning in Mind*, ed. B. Loewer and G. Rey. Oxford: Blackwell. (Reprinted in Perry 1993B)

1991b. Actions and Movements. With David Israel and Syun Tutiya. *Proceedings of ICAI-'91*. Mountain View: Morgan Kaufmann.

1991c. Il Filosofo e il computer. *Informatica e Scienze Umane: Lo Stato ADell'Arte*, ed. L. Gallino. Milan: Franco Angeli.

1991d. Information and Architecture. With David Israel. *Situation Theory and Its Applications*, ed. J. Barwise, J. M. Gawron, G. Plotkin, and S. Tutiya. Vol. 2. Stanford University: CSLI.

1993a. Williams on the Self and Its Future. *Introduction to Philosophy*, ed. J. Perry and M. Bratman. 2nd ed. New York: Oxford University Press. (Reprinted in Perry 2002B1)

1993b. Executions, Motivations and Accomplishments. With David Israel and Syun Tutiya. *The Philosophical Review* 102:515–40.

1993c. Richly Grounded Symbols in ASL. With E. Macken and C. Haas. *Sign Language Studies* 81:375–394.

1994a. Fodor and Lepore on Holism. *Philosophical Studies* 73:123–138.

1994b. Davidson's Sentences and Wittgenstein's Builders. Presidential Address, *Proceedings and Addresses of the American Philosophical Association* 68:23–37. Reprinted in the enlarged edition of Perry 1993B.

1994c. Introduction. *Berkeley*'s *Three Dialogues*, ed. D. Hilbert and J. Perry. Claremont: Arete Press.

1994d. Intentionality and Its Puzzles. *A Companion to the Philosophy of Mind*, ed. S. Guttenplan. Oxford: Blackwell.

1995. American Sign Language and Heterogeneous Communication Systems. With E. Macken and C. Haas. *Sign Language Studies* 89:363–412.

1996a. Evading the Slingshot. *Philosophy and Cognitive Science: Categories, Consciousness, and Reasoning*, ed. A. Clark, J. Ezquerro, and J. Larrazabal. Dordrecht: Kluwer Academic Publishers. (Reprinted in the enlarged edition of Perry 1993B)

1996b. Interfacing Situations. With E. Macken. *Logic, Language and Computation*, ed. J. Seligman and D. Westerstahl. Vol. 1. Stanford: CSLI Publications.

1996c. Where Monsters Dwell. *Logic, Language and Computation*, ed. J. Seligman and D. Westerstahl. Vol. 1. Stanford: CSLI Publications.

1996d. Self. *The Encyclopedia of Philosophy, Supplement*. New York: Simon & Schuster Macmillan.

1996e. Indexicals. *The Encyclopedia of Philosophy, Supplement*. New York: Simon & Schuster Macmillan.

1996f. Philosophy of Mind. *Microsoft Encarta Encyclopedia*. Redmond, Wash.: Microsoft Corporation.

1996g. Reflexivity, Indexicality and Names. *Korean Journal of Cognitive Science* 7:95–112. (Reprinted in the enlarged edition of Perry 1993B)

1997a. Indexicals and Demonstratives. *Companion to the Philosophy of Language*, ed. R. Hale and C. Wright. Oxford: Blackwell.

1997b. Russell's *The Problems of Philosophy*: An Introduction to Bertrand Russell, *The Problems of Philosophy*. New York: Oxford University Press.

1997c. Reflexivity, Indexicality and Names. *Direct Reference, Indexicality and Proposition Attitudes*, ed. W. Künne, M. Anduschus, and A. Newen. Stanford: CSLI. (Reprinted in the enlarged edition of Perry 1993B)

1997d. Rip Van Winkle and Other Characters. *The European Review of Analytical Philosophy* 2:13–39. (Reprinted in the enlarged edition of Perry 1993B)

1997e. Disability, Inability and Cyberspace. With E. Macken, N. Scott, and J. McKinley. *Designing Computers for People–Human Values and the Design of Computer Technology*, ed. B. Friedman. Stanford: CSLI.

1997f. Possible Worlds Semantics. *Routledge Encyclopedia of Philosophy*. London: Routledge.

1997g. Situation Semantics. *Routledge Encyclopedia of Philosophy*. London: Routledge.

1998a. Broadening the Mind: Review of Jerry Fodor, *The Elm and The Expert*. *Philosophy and Phenomenological Research* 58:223–31. (Reprinted in the enlarged edition of Perry 1993B)

1998b. Contexts and Unarticulated Constituents. *Proceedings of the 1995 CSLI-Amsterdam Logic, Language and Computation Conference*. Stanford: CSLI.

1998c. Myself and I. *Philosophie in Synthetischer Absicht*, ed. M. Stamm. Stuttgart: Klett-Cotta. (Translated into German as *Mein Selbst und 'Ich'* by V. Friesen and A. Newen in *Selbst und Gehirn*, ed. A. Newen and K. Vogeley. Paderborn: mentis 2000. Reprinted in the enlarged edition of Perry 1993B.)

1999. Prolegomena to a Theory of Disability, Inability and Handicap. With D. Israel and E. Macken. *Logic, Language and Computation*. Vol. 2, ed. L. Moss, J. Ginzburg, and M. de Rijke. Stanford: CSLI.

2001a. Time, Consciousness and the Knowledge Argument. *The Importance of Time*, ed. L. N. Oaklander. Dordrecht: Kluwer.

2001b. Frege on Identity, Cognitive Value and Subject Matter. *Building on Frege: New Essays about Sense, Content, and Concept*, ed. A. Newen, U. Nortmann, and R. Stuhlmann-Laeisz. Stanford: CSLI.

2002a. The Two Faces of Identity. *Identity, Personal Identity and the Self*. Indianapolis: Hackett Publishing. (Perry 2002B1)

2002b. Information, Action, and Persons. *Identity, Personal Identity and the Self*. Indianapolis: Hackett Publishing. (Perry 2002B1)

2002c. The Self, Self-Knowledge, and Self-Notions. *Identity, Personal Identity and the Self*. Indianapolis: Hackett Publishing. (Perry 2002B1)

2002d. The Sense of Identity. *Identity, Personal Identity and the Self*. Indianapolis: Hackett Publishing. (Perry 2002B1)

2002e. Review of Gilles Fauconner and Mark Turner, The Way We Think: Conceptual Blending and the Minds Hidden Complexities. *The American Scientist* 90:576–78.

2003a. Predelli's threatening note: contexts, utterances, and tokens in the philosophy of language. *Journal of Pragmatics* 35:373–87.

2003b. The Subject Matter Fallacy. *Journal of Applied Logic* 1:93–105.

2004a. Precis of Knowledge, Possibility and Consciousness. *Philosophy and Phenomenological Research* 68:172–81.

2004b. Reply to Critics. *Philosophy and Phenomenological Research* 68:207–28.

2004c. Compatibilist Options. *Freedom and Determinism*, ed. J. K. Campbell, M. O'Rourke, and D. Shier. Cambridge, Mass.: MIT Press.

2005. Personal Identity, Memory and the Self. *Synergies: Interdisciplinary Communications*, ed. W. Østreng, 16–25. Oslo: Center for Advanced Study.

2006a. Using Indexicals. *The Blackwell Guide to the Philosophy of Language*, ed. M. Devitt and R. Hanley, 314–34. Oxford: Blackwell.

2006b. Mary and Max and Jack and Ned. *Oxford Studies in Metaphysics II*, ed. D. Zimmermann, 79–90. Oxford: Oxford University Press.

2006c. Three Demonstrations and a Funeral. With K. Korta. *Mind and Language* 21:166–86.

2006d. How Real are Future Events? *Time and History. Proceedings of the 28th International Wittgenstein Symposium, Kirchberg am Wesel, Austria, 2005*, ed. F. Stadler and M. Stöltzner, 13–30. Ontos: Frankfurt a.M.

2006e. Stalnaker and Indexical Belief. *Content and Modality: Themes from the Philosophy of Robert Stalnaker*, ed. J. Thompson and A. Byrne, 204–21. Oxford: Oxford University Press.

2006f. Pragmatics. With K. Korta. *The Stanford Encycopedia of Philosophy*. URL: http://plato.stanford.edu/

2006g. Varieties of Minimalist Semantics. With K. Korta. *Philosophy and Phenomenological Research* 73:451–9.

2007a. Radical minimalism, moderate contextualism. With K. Korta. *Context-Sensitivity and Semantic Minimalism. New Essays on Semantics and Pragmatics*, ed. G. Preyer and G. Peter, 94–111. Oxford: Oxford University Press.

2007b. How to Say Things with Words. With K. Korta. *John Searle's Philosophy of Language: Force, Meaning, and Thought*, ed. S. L. Tsohatzidis, 169–89, Cambridge, Mass.: Cambridge University Press.

2007c. Situating Semantics: A Response. *Situating Semantics. Essays on the Philosophy of John Perry,* ed. M. O'Rourke and C. Washington, 507–75 Cambridge, Mass.: MIT.

2008. The Pragmatic Circle. With K. Korta. *Synthese* 165:347–357.

2009. Reference: A new paradigm. With K. Korta. *Meaning, Content and Argument*, ed. J. M. Larrazabal and L. Zubeldia, 73–88. Bilbao: UPV-EHU.

2010a. Intentions to refer. With K. Korta. *Meaning and context.* ed, L. Baptista and E. Rast, 161–186 Bern: Peter Lang.

2010b. What is said. With K. Korta. *Context-Dependence, Perspective and Relativity,* ed. F. Recanati, I. Stojanovic, and N. Villanueva, 51–67. Berlin: de Gruyter.

References

Adams, C. 2004. Can You get Amnesia from a Blow to the Head? *The Straight Dope*. http://www.straightdope.com/columns/read/2504/can-you-get-amnesia-from-a-blow-to-the-head.

Almog, J., Perry, J., and Wettstein, H. 1989. *Themes from Kaplan*. New York: Oxford University Press.

Ayer, A. J. 1936. *Language, Truth, and Logic*. London: Gollancz.

Bailey, A. 2006. Zombies, Epiphenomenalism, and Physicalist Theories of Consciousness. *Canadian Journal of Philosophy* 36:481–509

Bailey, A. 2009. Zombies and Epiphenomenalism. *Dialogue* 48:129–144.

Bach, K. 2004. Minding the Gap. *The Semantics/Pragmatics Distinction*, ed. C. Bianchi, 27–43. Stanford: CSLI.

Bach, K. 2006. The Excluded Middle: Semantic Minimalism without Minimal Propositions. *Philosophy and Phenomenological research* 73:435–42.

Bach, K. 2007. Reflections on *Reference and Reflexivity*. *Situating Semantics. Essays on the Philosophy of John Perry*, ed. M. O'Rourke and C. Washington, 395-424. Cambridge, Mass: MIT Press.

Barwise, J. 1988. On the Circumstantial Relation between Meaning and Content. *Meaning and Mental Representations*, ed. U. Eco, M. Santambrogio, and P. Violi, 23–39. Bloomington: Indiana University Press.

Borg, E. 2005. Saying What You Mean. *Ellipsis and Non-Sentential Speech,* ed. R. Elugardo and R. Stainton, 237–62. Dordrecht: Springer.

Bühler, K. 1934. *Sprachtheorie. Die Darstellungsfunktion der Sprache*. Jena: Fischer. (2nd ed.: 1965)

Butler, J. 1736. Of Personal Identity. Dissertation 1 of *The Analogy of Religion, Natural and Revealed, to the Constitution and Course of Nature (with Dissertations)*. (Reprinted in Perry 1975E: 99–105)

Castañeda, H.-N. 1989. *Thinking, Language, and Experience*. Minneapolis: University of Minnesota Press.

Cappelen, H. and Lepore, E. 2005. *Insensitive Semantics: A Defense of Semantic Minimalism and Speech Act Pluralism.* Oxford: Blackwell.

Cappelen, H. and Lepore, E. 2007. The Myth of Unarticulated Constituents. *Situating Semantics. Essays on the Philosophy of John Perry*, ed. M. O'Rourke and C. Washington, 199–214. Cambridge, Mass.: MIT Press.

Carnap, R. 1960. *Meaning and Necessity. A Study in Semantics and Modal Logic.* Chicago: University of Chicago Press.

Carston, R. 2002. *Thoughts and Utterances. The Pragmatics of Explicit Communication.* Oxford: Blackwell.

Chalmers, D. 2004a. Imagination, Indexicality, and Intensions. *Philosophy and Phenomenological Research* 68:182–90.

Chalmers, D. 2004b. Response to Perry's Reply. http://consc.net/papers/perry.html-#response

Chastain, C. 1975. Reference and Context. *Minnesota Studies in the Philosophy of Science: Language, Mind, and Knowledge* 7:194–269.

Clark, H. H. 1996. *Using Language*. Cambridge: Cambridge University Press.

Corazza, E. 2004. *Reflecting the Mind: Indexicality and Quasi-Indexicality*. Oxford: Oxford University Press.

Corazza, E. 2011. Revisiting Millianism. Draft.

Corazza, E. and Dokic, J. 2010. Situated Minimalism versus Free Enrichment. *Synthese*. Online.

Cresswell, M. 1973. *Logics and Languages*. London: Methuen.

Davidson, D. 1967. Meaning and Truth. *Synthese* 17:304–23.

Donnellan, K. 1966. Reference and Definite Descriptions. *Philosophical Review* 75:281–304.

Donnellan, K. 1970. Proper Names and Identifying Descriptions. *Synthese* 21:335–58.

Donnellan, K. 1974. Speaking of Nothing. *Philosophical Review* 83:3–31.

Dretske, F. 1981. *Knowledge and the Flow of Information*. Cambrigde, Mass.: MIT Press.

Frege, Gottlob. 1879. *Begriffsschrift*. (Translated as: Concept Script, a formal language of pure thought modelled upon that of arithmetic. *From Frege to Gödel: A Source Book in Mathematical Logic, 1879-1931*, ed. J. van Heijenoort. Cambridge, Mass.: Harvard University Press 1967.)

Frege, G. 1892. Über Sinn und Bedeutung. *Zeitschrift für Philosophie und philosophische Kritik* 100:25–50. (Translated as: On *Sinn* and *Bedeutung*. *The Frege Reader*, ed. M. Beaney. Oxford: Blackwell, 151–171)

Frege, G. 1915. My Basic Logical Insights. *The Frege Reader*, ed. M. Beaney, 321–24. Oxford: Blackwell 1997.

Frege, G. 1918. Thought. *The Frege Reader*, ed. M. Beaney, 325–345. Oxford: Blackwell 1997.

Frege, G. 1976. *Nachgelassene Schriften und wissenschaftlicher Briefwechsel*, Vol. 2, ed. G. Gabriel. Hamburg: Meiner.

Frege, G. 1979. *Posthumous Writings*, ed. H. Hermes, F. Kambartel, and F. Kaulbach. Oxford: Blackwell.

Geach, P. 1962. *Reference and Generality*. Ithaca: Cornell University Press.

Geach, P. 1967. Identity. *Review of Metaphysics* 21:3–12.

Geach P. 1972. *Logic Matters*. Berkeley: University of California Press.

Gibson, J. J. 1979. *The Ecological Approach to Visual Perception*. Boston: Houghton Mifflin.

Gödel, Kurt. 1944. Russell's mathematical logic. *The Philosophy of Bertrand Russell*, ed. P. A. Schilpp, 122–53. Evanston/Chicago: Northwestern University Press.

Gordon, R. 1995. Simulation Without Introspection or Inference from Me to You. *Mental Simulation,* ed. M. Davies and T. Stone. Oxford: Blackwell.

Grice, H. P. 1941. Personal Identity. *Mind* 50:330–50.

Grice, H. P. 1975. Logic and conversation. *Syntax and Semantics*, ed. P. Cole and J. Morgan. Vol. 3, 41–58. New York: Academic Press.

Grice, H. P. 1989. *Studies in the Way of Words*. Cambridge, Mass.: Harvard University Press.

Heim, I. and Kratzer, A. 1998. *Semantics in Generative Grammar.* Oxford: Blackwell.

Hintikka, J. 1962. *Knowledge and Belief: An Introduction to the Logic of the Two Notions*. Cornell: Cornell University Press.

Hintikka, J. 1967. Individuals, Possible Worlds, and Epistemic Logic. *Noûs* 1:33–62.

Hume, D. 1741. Of Personal Identity. *A Treatise of Human Nature.* Part 4, Section 6. (Reprinted in Perry 1975E: 161–72)

van Inwagen, P. 1990. *Material Beings*. Ithaca: Cornell University Press

Jackson, F. 1997. What Mary Didn't Know. *Journal of Philosophy* 83:291–295.

Kamp, H. and Partee, B. 2004. *Context-dependence in the Analysis of Linguistic Meaning*. Amsterdam: Elsevier.

Kaplan, D. 1989a. Demonstratives. *Themes from Kaplan*, ed. J. Almog, J. Perry, and H. Wettstein, 481–563. Oxford: Oxford University Press.

Kaplan, D. 1989b. Afterthoughts. *Themes from Kaplan*, ed. J. Almog, J. Perry, and H. Wettstein, 565–614. Oxford: Oxford University Press.

Kirk, R. 1974a. Sentience and Behaviour. *Mind* 83:43–60.

Kirk, R. 1974b. Zombies v. Materialists. *Supplementary Proceedings of the Aristotelian Society* 48:135–52.

Kratzer, A. 2007. Situations in natural language semantics. *Stanford Encyclopedia of Philosophy*, ed. E. N. Zalta.
URL = http://plato.stanford.edu/archives/spring2007/entries/situations-semantics/

Kratzer, A. 2011. *Modals and Conditionals: New and Revized Perspectives.* Oxford: Oxford University Press.

Kripke, S. 1963. Semantical considerations on modal logic. *Acta Philosophica Fennica* 16:83–94.

Kripke, S. 1977. Speaker Reference and Semantic Reference. *Midwest Studies in Philosophy* 2:255–277.

Kripke, S. 1979. A puzzle about belief. *Meaning and Use*, ed. A. Margalit, 239–283. Dordrecht: Reidel.

Kripke, S. 1980. *Naming and Necessity*. Oxford: Blackwell. (First published in *Semantics of Natural Language*, ed. D. Davidson and G. Harman. Dordrecht: Reidel 1972)

Künne, W. 1992. Hybrid Proper Names. *Mind* 101:721—31.

Lewis, D. 1970. General Semantics. *Synthese* 22:18–67.

Lewis, D. 1976. Survival and Identity. *The Identities of Persons*, ed. A. Rorty, 17–40. Berkeley: University of California Press.

Lewis, D. 1984. Putnam's Paradox. *Australasian Journal of Philosophy* 62:221–236.

Lewis, D. 1990. What Experience Teaches. *Mind and Cognition*, ed. W. Lycan, 499–519. Oxford: Blackwell.

Loar, B. 1990. Phenomenal States. *Philosophical Perspectives* 4:81–108

Locke, J. 1694. Of Identity and Diversity. *Essay Concerning Human Understanding*, 2nd edition, Book 2, Chapter 27. (Reprinted in Perry 1975E: 33–52)

Lycan, W. G. 1995. A Limited Defense of Phenomenal Information. *Conscious Experience*, ed. T. Metzinger, 243–258. Paderborn: Schöningh.

Mach, E. 1914. *The Analysis of Sensations*, ed. S. Waterlow, tr. C. M. Williams. Chicago/London: Open Court.

Martí, G. 1995. The Essence of Genuine Reference. *Journal of Philosophical Logic* 24:275–289.

Mellor, D. H. 1995. *The Facts of Causation*. London: Routledge.

Mill, J. S. 1893. *A System of Logic*. London: Longman, Green & Co.

Millikan, R. G. 1993. The Myth of the Essential Indexical. *White Queen Psychology and Other Essays for Alice*. Cambridge, Mass.: MIT Press.

Montague, R. 1970a. English as a formal language. *Formal Philosophy: Selected Papers by Richard Montagu,* ed. R. Thomason, 188–221. New Haven: Yale University Press.

Montague, R. 1970b. The proper treatment of quantification in ordinary English. *Formal Philosophy: Selected Papers by Richard Montague,* ed. R. Thomason, 222–46. New Haven: Yale University Press.

Mulligan, K. and Smith, B. 1986. A Husserlian Theory of Indexicality. *Grazer Philosophische Studien* 28:133–163.

Neale, S. 2007. On Location. *Situating Semantics. Essays on the Philosophy of John Perry,* ed. M. O'Rourke and C. Washington, 251–393. Cambridge, Mass.: MIT Press.

Nemirow, L. 1990. Physicalism and the Cognitive Role of Acquaintance. *Mind and Cognition*, ed. W. Lycan, 490–499. Oxford: Blackwell.

Olson, E. T. 1997a. Was I ever a Fetus? *Philosophy and Phenomenological Research* 57:95–110.

Olson, E. T. 1997b. *The Human Animal: Personal Identity Without Psychology*. Oxford: Oxford University Press.

O'Rourke, M. and Washington, C. 2007. *Situating Semantics. Essays on the Philosophy of John Perry*. Cambridge, Mass.: MIT Press.

Papineau, D. 2002. *Thinking about Consciousness*. Oxford: Oxford University Press.

Parfit, D. 1971. Personal Identity. *Philosophical Review* 80:3–27.

Partee, B. 1997. Montague Grammar. *The Handbook of Logic and Language,*. ed. J. v. Benthem and A. ter Meulen, 5–91. Amsterdam: Elsevier.

Recanati, F. 1993. *Direct Reference: From Language to Thought*. Oxford: Blackwell.

Recanati, F. 2000. *Oratio Obliqua. Oratia recta: An essay on metarepresentation.* Cambridge, Mass.: MIT Press.

Recanati, F. 2002. Unarticulated Constituents. *Linguistics and Philosophy* 25:299–345.

Recanati, F. 2004. *Literal Meaning*. Cambridge: Cambridge University Press.

Recanati, F. 2007a. It is Raining (Somewhere). *Linguistics and Philosophy* 30:123–46

Recanati, F. 2007b. *Perspectival Thought*. Oxford: Oxford University Press.

Recanati, F., Stojanovic, I., and Villanueva, N. 2010. *Context-Dependence, Perspective and Relativity*. Berlin: Mouton de Gruyter.

Reid, T. 1785. *Essays on the Intellectual Power of Man*. Essay III: Of Memory, Chapters 5 and 6. (Reprinted in Perry 1975E, 107–18)

Richard, M. 1983. Direct reference and ascriptions of belief. *Journal of Philosophical Logic* 12:425–452.

Richard, M. 1990. *Propositional Attitudes: An Essay on Thoughts and How We Ascribe Them*. Cambridge: Cambridge University Press.

Russell, B. 1904. Correspondence with Frege. *Propositions and Attitudes*, ed. N. Salmon and S. Soames, 57. Oxford: Oxford University Press.

Russell, B. 1918. *The Philosophy of Logical Atomism*. Chicago: Open Court 1985.

Shoemaker, S. 1963. *Self-Knowledge and Self-Identity*. Ithaca: Cornell University Press.

Shoemaker, S. 1970. Persons and Their Pasts. *American Philosophical Quarterly* 7:269–85.

Shoemaker, S. 1997. Self and Substance. *Philosophical Perspectives* 11:283–319.

Shoemaker, S. 1999. Self, Body, and Coincidence. *Supplementary Proceedings of the Aristotelian Society* 73:287–306.

Smart, J. J. C. 1959. Sensations and Brain Processes. *The Philosophical Review* 68:141–56.

Soames, S. 1995. Beyond singular propositions. *Canadian Journal of Philosophy* 25:515-49.

Sperber, D. and Wilson, D. 1986. *Relevance. Communication and Cognition*. Oxford: Blackwell. (2nd expanded and revised ed.: 1995)

Stanley, J. 2000. Context and Logical Form. *Linguistics and Philosophy* 23 (4):391–434.

Stanley, J. 2002. Making it Articulated. *Mind and Language* 17:149–68.

Strawson, P. F. 1950. On Referring. *Mind* 59: 320–44.

Taylor, K. 2001. Sex, Breakfast and Descriptus Interruptus. *Synthese* 128:45–61.

Taylor, K. 2007. Misplaced Modification and the Illusion of Opacity. *Situating Semantics. Essays on the Philosophy of John Perry*, ed. M. O'Rourke and C. Washington, 215-50. Cambridge, Mass.: MIT Press.

Wettstein, H. 1986. Has Semantics Rested on a Mistake? *Journal of Philosophy* 83:185–209.

Williams, B. 1956–57. Personal Identity and Individuation. *Proceedings of the Aristotelian Society* 57:229–252.

Williams, B. 1970. The Self and the Future. *Philosophical Review* 79:161–180.

Williams, B. 1973. *Problems of the Self.* Cambridge: Cambridge University Press.